P9-CQK-431

HOW THE EBOOKS WORK

The eBooks are provided in EPUB file format. Please note that you will need an eBook reader installed on your device to open the file. Many devices come with this as standard, but you may still need to install one manually from Google Play.

The eBook content is identical to the content in the printed guide.

HOW TO DOWNLOAD THE WALKING EYE APP

1. Download the Walking Eye App from the App Store or Google Play.
2. Open the app and select the scanning function from the main menu.
3. Scan the QR code on this page – you will then be asked a security question to verify ownership of the book.
4. Once this has been verified, you will see your eBook in the purchased ebook section, where you will be able to download it.

Other destination apps and eBooks are available for purchase separately or are free with the purchase of the Insight Guide book.

TOP 10 ATTRACTIONS

TORRE DOS CLÉRIGOS
Porto's lofty landmark, with a 225-step hike up the Baroque tower for the best city views. See page 46.

PORT WINE CELLARS
Tour the cellars in Vila Nova de Gaia and sample Porto's most famous tipple. See page 66.

THE SÉ
The city's imposing hill-top cathedral offers a panorama of the city. See page 35.

IGREJA DE SÃO FRANCISCO
The austere church facade belies a breathtaking interior of Baroque gilded woodcarving. See page 33.

PALÁCIO DA BOLSA
Historic home of the Stock Exchange, with an opulent interior. See page 32.

JARDIM DO PALÁCIO DE CRISTAL
Romantic gardens, with sensational river views. Perfect for a picnic or family outing. See page 57.

ESTAÇÃO DE SÃO BENTO
A feast of *azulejos* (tiles) depicting historical scenes adorns the entrance hall of the city's central station. See page 41.

LELLO
One of the world's most beautiful bookshops, with Harry Potter links. See page 48.

SERRALVES
A must for art lovers: contemporary art museum and Art Deco mansion in beautiful park surrounds. See page 64.

CITY OF BRIDGES
Leisurely one-hour river cruises under the bridges give superb views of the city. See page 73.

A PERFECT DAY

9.00am

Breakfast
Kick off the day with coffee, eggs and croissants at the lovely Mercador Café in Rua das Flores. Stroll along this appealing street with its grand mansions and enticing shops.

12.00pm

Sé to Ribeira
Walk down the main street for the Sé (Cathedral) and admire the sweeping city views from the esplanade. Take a brief look at the cathedral and cloisters before heading down the steps to the right of the Episcopal Palace. A stairway leads all the way to the Ribeira but if you run out of puff a free lift makes light work of the steepest section.

11.00am

A feast of *azulejos*
Drop down Rua dos Clérigos for the Praça da Liberdade, civic heart of the city. The broad Avenida dos Aliados stretches grandly up to the Town Hall. Beyond the Praça you'll find São Bento railway station, its entrance hall bedecked with 20,000 *azulejos* (tiles) illustrating scenes of Portuguese history and traditions.

10.00am

Top of the tower
Visit the nearby Clérigos Church and Tower (see page 45). Climb 225 steps up the tower for the best views of the city, then take a peek inside the beautiful Baroque church.

1.30pm

Quayside cafés
From the Ribeira waterfront take the Dom Luís I bridge to Vila Nova de Gaia. Choose from the river-view cafés or grab a gourmet snack from the new Mercado Beira Rio just back from the waterfront.

IN **PORTO**

4.00pm

Jardim do Morro

Take the cable car up to the Jardim do Morro (gardens) for fabulous views of the river, Dom Luís I bridge and Porto, and even better ones if you climb up to the belvedere of the Serra do Pilar Monastery.

10.00pm

Hit the galerias

Party with the locals in the bar-packed streets in and around Rua da Galeria de Paris, then dance the night away at Café au Lait (No. 46) or Plano B (Rua Cândido dos Reis, 30).

5.30pm

Aperitivo time

Return to Porto and stroll along the scenic Ribeira quayside, and choose a pavement café for a *porto tónico* (white port and tonic on ice), looking across at the port lodges on the left bank.

2.30pm

Port galore

Follow lunch with a tour and tasting in one or more of the many port wine cellars (see page 67).

8.00pm

Trusty taverna

Try local specialities at Adega de São Nicolau (see page 108), a cosy cellar restaurant back from the waterfront at the western end of Cais da Ribeira.

CONTENTS

INTRODUCTION

For centuries Portugal's second city has been synonymous with port, but thanks to its recent renaissance, Porto offers far more than the famous ruby tipple. Once an industrial, work-manlike city, it now claims a revitalised cultural scene and is fascinating in its own right.

Hugging the steep banks where the River Douro spills into the Atlantic, much of the city's appeal lies in its location. Ever since the Romans established a trading route here Porto has prospered from commerce. It was here that Prince Henry the Navigator (1394–1460) learned his love of ships and initiated

⊙ THE RIVER DOURO

Flowing all the way from northern Spain, the River Douro has long been the source of Porto's wealth. It is the third longest river of the Iberian Peninsula, flowing 900km (559 miles) from its source, near Duruelo de la Sierra in Spain, to the Atlantic at Porto. Upstream from the city the river winds through the steep and scenic terraced vineyards of the Douro Valley, famous for the country's centuries-old port wine. Traditionally the wine was shipped in oak barrels on *barcos rabelos* (flat-bottomed, square-sailed boats) to be stored in the cool port-wine lodges of Vila Nova de Gaia, across the river from Porto. This was a hazardous journey, with *rabelos* having to navigate the often shallow, fast-flowing waters of the Upper Douro. These colourful craft are no longer used commercially (the wine is now transported, less ro-mantically, by truck) but you can often see replica *rabelo* boats on the quayside in Porto, with wine barrels on board.

Portugal's role as one of the primary players in the Age of Discovery. Porto, where some of the caravels were constructed, prospered from the new sources of wealth. Later the port wine trade with Britain was to compensate for the loss of the lucrative spice trade. Today the city is still the hub of the port wine industry, and continued English involvement can be seen in the conspicuous names of the

Porto from the air

shippers and brands above the port wine lodges.

HISTORIC PORTO

With dramatic bridges, Baroque churches and a red-roofed jumble of buildings creeping up the hillside, Porto contains a wonderful cocktail of architecture. It poses majestically on steep slopes, with myriad *miradouros* (look-out points) affording superb views across the river to Vila Nova de Gaia, where the famous cellars nurture the precious port wine. Soaring above the city in the centre is the Baroque Torre de Clérigos, the 75-metre (246ft) -high bell tower of the eponymous church, while towards the river the Sé (Cathedral) crowns the Penaventosa hill. Dotted around are the towers of Baroque churches, whose sober facades belie a wealth of lavish gilded woodwork inside. These Baroque monuments were happily left unscathed by the great earthquake of 1755 which ripped through the city of Lisbon.

The real tourist magnet of the city is the Ribeira quarter, a World Heritage Site where multi-coloured houses tumble down to the River Douro and a string of restaurants spill out on to the boat-lined quayside. Behind the waterfront lies a labyrinth of steep cobbled alleys and stairways, where washing billows from flower-filled balconies. Renovation and gentrification is underway but this historic quarter still has an authentic medieval feel. Linking Ribeira with Vila Nova de Gaia across the River Douro is the great swoop of the Ponte Dom Luís I, the most central and iconic of the city's six bridges.

PORTO V LISBON

According to an old Portuguese saying *'Porto works while Lisbon plays, Coimbra studies and Braga prays'*. Porto is proud of its mercantile heritage and the fact that it gives its name not only to the famous fortified wine but also to the nation (it was called Portus Cale, the port of Cale, by the Romans – which gave rise to Portucale and hence Portugal). The city has always worked hard and it is still a major commercial centre. The work ethic could have something to do with the climate. Porto lies in northwest Portugal, 314km (195 miles) north of Lisbon and only 3km (1.5miles) from the Atlantic. While palm trees and bird-of-paradise flowers flourish on its hillsides, it has a cooler climate than Lisbon (heat waves are rare) and the rains are quite abundant (1,150mm/45ins per year), especially from November to March.

Like Lisbon, Porto is clustered on hills overlooking a river, but unlike the capital, with its pastel walls and Mediterranean light, Porto is in many ways a northern European city, with granite buildings (though softened by red-tile roofs) and hidden Baroque treasures. It is grittier and less polished than Lisbon, but is catching up with the capital fast, particularly when it comes to cuisine, accommodation and shopping. The city is known as 'the capital of the north', and with a population of 238,000 (or 1.8 million including the metropolitan area) it is the second largest city in Portugal.

PORTO'S RENAISSANCE

Less than 20 years ago Porto had a reputation for being a closed, mysterious city, its centre deserted and offering little of cultural interest. But recent years have seen a dramatic transformation, with spruced-up streets and a new sense of vitality. The regeneration goes on, and the city's modern landmarks include the lofty yellow cranes which punctuate the skyscape.

This increasingly cosmopolitan city is now a centre of arts, fashion and nightlife, with an undeniably youthful vibe. New bars and restaurants seem to open daily, along with hostels,

Porto Sunday Sessions brings music to City Park

hotels and Airbnbs to cater for the ever-increasing number of visitors. Art is no longer restricted to the treasures in museums and churches; there are dozens of cutting-edge galleries in its hip art neighbourhood, eye-catching street art is adding colour and life to previously abandoned quarters, while art festivals, music and modern architecture are thriving. The food scene is flourishing too, with Michelin-starred restaurants and trendy tapas bars joining the traditional tavernas.

It is hardly surprising that Porto is a rising star on the short-break scene. The city has been named European Best Destination no less than three times (2012, 2014 and 2017). The airport has been expanded to cater for direct flights from North America and Canada, and there are dozens of flights with low-cost carriers from other European cities. The award-winning cruise terminal at

Gourmet octopus dish

the port of Leixões, opened in 2015, is bringing ever greater numbers of visitors.

But at the same time Porto still has the feel of a provincial city, known above all for the charm of its labyrinthine streets, the beauty of its hand-painted *azulejos* (tiles) and the occasional ornate architectural flourish. Vintage trams still rattle along its steep lanes, washing hangs on crumbling facades and old timers still enjoy a port wine in the older cafés or tuck into gargantuan dishes of beans and tripe. Porto has changed with the times but retains an old world charm.

> ### 'Porto' or 'Oporto'?
>
> If you want to sound like a local call the city 'Porto'. This has always been the local name but during the heady days of the port wine trade the British called it Oporto. The added 'O' is just the article which is placed before the name Porto, but the British thought it was part of the name and called it Oporto.

BEYOND THE CITY

Monuments to former splendours, a beautiful cityscape and a delectable signature tipple are not the end of the city's charms. From here you can also visit the upper reaches of the Douro Valley, following the river on the trail of the wine boats, taking the scenic rail route or hiring a car and staying a night or two at one of the *quintas* (wine estates) to tour the vineyards and wineries. Also within easy reach by rail or car are the historic cities of Braga and Guimarães in northern Portugal and, to the south, the university city of Coimbra. Then there's the seaside, just down the road from Porto, with big sweeping views of the ocean and surfers. A vintage tram trundles alongside the river to Foz do Douro where the river meets the ocean, or a bus or metro will take you to Matosinhos for gorgeous sunsets and the freshest of fish.

A BRIEF HISTORY

The Porto region has been inhabited for over three millennia, but it was the Romans who established the city of Portus on the right bank of the River Douro, and Cale facing it across the water. These twin cities gave rise to the dialect name 'Portucale', the origin of 'Portugal'; Porto is the city that gave its name to the nation as well as to the well-known fortified wine.

EARLY SETTLERS

Since the days of the first settlers the fortunes of Porto have been linked with its location at the mouth of the River Douro where it empties into the Atlantic. The earliest recorded settlers were of Celtic origin and a few relics of their civilisation have been discovered in the heart of Porto; otherwise there are scant signs of early dwellers. Under Roman rule from the second century BC the city played an important role on the main trade route between Lisbon and Braga.

With the collapse of the Roman Empire, barbarian tribes invaded from northern Europe. In the 5th century the Germanic Suevi (Swabians) settled in Galicia, ruling from Braga and annexing much of the peninsula. Suevi rule was superseded by the Visigoths in 469, and control of the region changed once again in 711 when the Moorish invasion overwhelmed most of the Iberian peninsula. The Christian War of Reconquest of the peninsula (the Reconquista in Portuguese) began in 718 and took root in the north. By 868 Portucale was established as a frontier against Muslim rule by the Christian warlord, Count Vimara Peres, who held sway over the entire area between the Minho to the north and the River Douro.

BIRTH OF A NATION

When Moorish power waned, 'Portucale' was just a small country of the Kingdom of León and Castile, centred on the Douro. It became independent after Afonso Henriques, the son of Henry of Burgundy, defeated the Moors at the Battle of Ourique in 1139 and named himself the first king of Portugal, Afonso I. By now he had captured Santarém and Lisbon, making his now royal realm the whole of present-day Portugal north of the River Tagus.

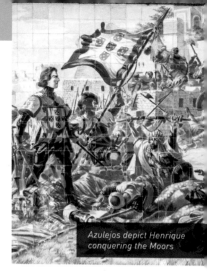

Azulejos depict Henrique conquering the Moors

The legitimate male line of Henry of Burgundy finally ended in 1385 when João of Avis, known as João the Good, won a decisive victory against the Castilians at the famous Battle of Ajubarrota, assuring him as King of Portugal and a new ruling dynasty. King João's troops had been assisted by English archers and the victory prompted the Treaty of Windsor in 1386, the diplomatic Anglo-Portuguese alliance. This was well and truly sealed when the king married Philippa of Lancaster, daughter of John of Gaunt. The wedding took place with great pomp and ceremony in the cathedral of Porto and the alliance remains the oldest of its kind in the world.

HENRY THE NAVIGATOR

King João and Philippa's fourth son, Henrique (1394–1460), was to change the map of the world. He is believed to have

Tripas à moda do Porto is still one of the city's iconic dishes

been born in Porto in the building now known as the Casa do Infante (House of the Prince, open to the public, see page 30). Known to the English as Henry the Navigator, he was famed as the founder and financier of Portugal's golden age of discovery. The launching point of his career was the daring capture of the Muslim North African city of Ceuta in 1415, with his father and brothers, putting an end to attacks by Barbary pirates on the Portuguese coast. For the venture against the Moors the people of Porto surrendered their finest cuts of meats to the navy and lived on tripe instead, thus earning them the nickname of *Tripeiros* or Tripe-eaters.

Henry was not in fact a navigator, but under his patronage Portuguese seamen founded the country's first colonies. In 1418 he moved south and established a school of navigation at Sagres, the desolate promontory in the southwest (the western tip of today's Algarve). Here he assembled a group of cartographers, astronomers, geographers and navigators to plot a sea route from Europe to India. Henry died in 1460 without finding the route to India, but Vasco da Gama's legendary sea voyage in 1497–99 paved the way for the Portuguese to establish their empire in Asia. The motivation for these voyages was partly religious, but largely commercial. By the time of his death in 1460 Henry had managed to establish a monopoly on all trade, including slavery, conducted along the African coast south of Cape Bojador.

In 1578 tragedy struck and altered the course of Portuguese history. The young King Sebastião was one of thousands killed at the Battle of Alcácer Quibir in a doomed attempt to invade Morocco. The death of the king led to the end of the Avis dynasty; Spain invaded in 1580, and it took 60 years for the Portuguese to organise a successful uprising against the occupation.

On 1 December 1640 – a date still celebrated as Portugal's Independence Day – Spanish rule was overthrown and the Duke of Bragança was crowned King João IV. His grandson, João V, enjoyed a long and glittering reign (1705–50) with wealth pouring in from gold discoveries in Brazil. It was during this time that many of Porto's church interiors were adorned with lavishly gilded woodwork.

NAPOLEONIC INVASIONS

In Porto, as in the rest of Portugal, the Peninsular War and its aftermath halted progress for nearly half a century. During the three Napoleonic invasions French troops took Porto twice, in 1808 and 1809; on the second occasion they were expelled by troops under the command of Arthur Wellesley, later the Duke of Wellington. On 29 March 1809 hundreds of fleeing residents drowned when the pontoon bridge across the Douro collapsed under their weight.

The Portuguese royal family had fled to Brazil in 1807, ahead of Napoleon's invading forces. At the end of the war King João VI declined to return to Portugal, giving rise to a complex series of political events and the 'War of the Two Brothers' in 1832–34, a fight for the Portuguese Crown between Miguel I for the Absolutists and Pedro IV (previously Emperor of Brazil) for the Liberals. Miguel and his troops besieged the Liberals in

⊘ PORT AND THE BRITISH FACTOR

Some say port was invented by British merchants looking to replace French claret, which was boycotted during wars with France in the 17th century. By adding a little brandy to the local red Douro, they found the wine sufficiently fortified to withstand temperature changes and long sea voyages. It also produced a fresh sweet flavour that deepened with age. Whoever invented it, port was a big hit with the British and became 'as British as roast beef'. The Methuen Treaty of 1703 opened English markets to Portuguese wines and the British shippers of Porto became increasingly rich and powerful. The next 30 years saw an unprecedented expansion of trade in the Upper Douro and in 1727 a Shippers' Association was established to regulate the trade and control prices paid to the Portuguese producers. The growth of trade gave rise to the famous port wine lodges spread over the hills of Vila Nova de Gaia. To combat the English stranglehold, the King of Portugal's Chief Minister, later the Marquês de Pombal, founded the Douro Wine Company in 1757 which restored a measure of Portuguese control. The Douro Valley became the world's first wine region with a legal demarcation and Porto and its region a main engine room of Portuguese expansion and commerce.

Porto for over a year. The war resulted in Miguel's exile and the restoration of liberalism, but further political strife followed. In September 1836 a democratic Chartists' group, which became known as the Septemberists, seized power but in turn split, with a royalist faction holding Lisbon and a republican junta holding Porto. A combined British and Spanish force, supporting the Quadruple Alliance of England, France, Spain and a royalist Portugal, received the surrender of the Porto junta in 1847.

Filled glasses at a port tasting

REGENERATION

In the second half of the 19th century the city saw a period of economic revival, industrialisation and urban expansion. The population soared as thousands of Portuguese from rural areas descended on the city. The first Industrial Exhibition of the Iberian Peninsula was held in 1865 at Porto's original Palácio de Cristal, a building inspired by London's Crystal Palace. An indication of the wealth of the city at the time was the creation of an ornate stock exchange, the Palacio da Bolsa (no longer functioning but open to the public). To keep up with growth, transport services were revitalised. In 1876 the French architect Gustav Eiffel designed the first railway bridge across the River Douro, the Ponte de Dona Maria Pia. Ten years later

Eiffel's former partner, Théophile Seyrig, designed the iconic Dom Luís I bridge and towards the end of the century electric trams were trundling through Porto.

FROM REPUBLIC TO REVOLUTION

In 1908 the reigning Portuguese king, Carlos I, and his eldest son, Luís Filipe, were assassinated in Lisbon. Two years later a republican revolution overthrew the monarchy. Portugal's last king, Manuel II, fled to England where he lived in exile, thus ending more than 750 years of monarchy. During the establishment of the Republic, Porto sustained its own democratic and republican leanings, and following the 1926 military coup Porto was the centre of liberal opposition to Salazar's lengthy dictatorship, which lasted until 1968. The city declined

The assassination of King Carlos I

in the 1960s, many citizens leaving the city for Foz do Douro or Matosinhos on the coast, and many Porto properties were left in serious disrepair.

The peaceful Carnation Revolution in 1974 finally ended the totalitarian regime. Led by army officers disaffected by the colonial wars in Africa, the revolution heralded a period of great celebration as Portugal emerged from decades of insularity. The years that followed were a period of both euphoria and political chaos.

MODERN PORTO

With its entry into the European Community (the forerunner to the EU) in 1986, Portugal became one of the fastest growing countries in Europe. Ten years later Porto was given a further boost with the designation of its historic centre as a Unesco World Heritage site, while winning the title of European Capital of Culture in 2001 gave rise to a major cultural programme, with the construction of new venues and a commitment to the regeneration of squares and streets. The Casa da Música was the most avant-garde addition to the city. But the economy began to stagnate and the 2008 financial crisis left Portugal with a budget deficit that was fast spiralling out of control. In 2011 it became the third EU country after Greece and Ireland to ask for a financial bail-out from the EU. It wasn't until

Porto metro travelling over the Dom Luís I bridge

2014, after harsh austerity measures had been implemented and the budget deficit reduced, that Portugal exited the bail-out programme.

Tourism has given Portugal a big economic boost in recent years, and accounts for around 10 percent of GDP. In 2017 the number of foreign tourists rose to a record 12.7 million, a rise of nearly 12% on 2016. Porto sees fewer tourists than Lisbon or the Algarve, but in 2017 was voted by travellers and tourism experts as Europe's Best Destination, having already been awarded the title twice before in 2012 and 2014. From 15 years ago when over half of its properties were in serious disrepair, the city has witnessed major regeneration, with new architecture, art galleries, chic shops, bars and restaurants.

In 2018 a city tax of €2 per person was introduced on all overnight stays in tourist accommodation. The money will be used to reduce the impact of the growing influx of visitors, in order to avoid tourism taking on the proportions of European destinations like Barcelona. As yet, tourism is not driving out the locals, but there are currently no restrictions on the number of hotels, bars and restaurants allowed to set up shop. It remains to be seen whether the historic heart of the city can preserve its local character and timeless charm.

HISTORICAL LANDMARKS

140BC Romans occupy the region and later found Portus Cale.

5th century AD Occupation by Visigoths.

711 Moors conquer the peninsula.

883 Northern Portugal (Portucale) regained by Christian forces.

1143 Portucale becomes the new Kingdom of Portugal. Afonso Henriques is the first king of Portugal.

1387 Dom João I and Philippa of Lancaster are married in the city's cathedral.

1415 Conquest of Ceuta under Henry the Navigator. Explorers reach Madeira, starting the Age of Discoveries.

1580 Portugal falls under Spanish rule for 60 years.

1703 Methuen Treaty between Portugal and England, which becomes known as the 'Port Wine Treaty'.

1808 and 1809 Napoleonic troops take Porto twice and are finally driven out in 1809 by Sir Arthur Wellesley (the future Wellington) in 1809.

1832-33 Siege of Porto.

1886 Opening of the Ponte Dom Luís I.

1887 Opening of Gustave Eiffel's Ponte Maria Pia railway bridge.

1891 Portugal's first republican revolution takes place in Porto.

1910 Creation of the Portuguese Republic.

1945 Opening of Porto's airport.

1974 Carnation Revolution, ending 48 years of António de Oliveira Salazar's fascist dictatorship.

1986 Portugal joins the European Community.

1996 Unesco World Heritage status granted to Ribeira.

2001 Porto is European Capital of Culture.

2002 First metro line opens.

2004 Portugal hosts EUFA European Football Championship. Estádio do Dragão is built.

2005 Ryanair introduces flights to Porto heralding the tourist boom.

2015 Award-winning cruise terminal opens at Leixões.

2018 Porto introduces controversial €2 tourist tax on overnight stays.

The pretty facades of Ribeira

WHERE TO GO

Provided you don't mind some steep hills and stairways, Porto is the perfect place to explore on foot. Most of the cultural attractions are packed into the old part of town and many areas are car-free. Streets are often narrow and not always marked on city maps, but if you do get lost there are always orientation points such as the omnipresent River Douro and the loftier bell towers. Alternatively, the friendly Portuenses (people from Porto) will point you in the right direction.

Outlying attractions are covered by bus, vintage trams or the metro. For visits to the cellars of the famous port wine lodges you can simply cross the Ponte Luis I bridge which spans the River Douro. For the seaside attractions of Foz do Douro it's just a case of hopping on a bus or tram.

The city is ideal for a weekend, but if you want to stroll through sleepy streets, linger over seafood dinners and learn about ruby and tawny ports, give it another day or two and savour it slowly.

RIBEIRA

Awarded Unesco World Heritage status in 1996, Ribeira (or Riverside) was one of the first areas of the city to be inhabited. It was the city's original trade hub, with boats off-loading their merchandise on the quayside. Today it is Porto at its most picturesque, with ancient arcades, coloured houses hugging the cliff and a warren of quiet narrow alleys behind. The river trade nowadays is purely for tourists, from one-hour cruises to see the 'city of bridges' to week-long trips up the Douro.

CAIS DA RIBEIRA

Like many areas of Porto, the **Cais da Ribeira** – or River Quayside – was not so long ago a crumbling and run-down quarter. Now it's vibrant and colourful, with a string of river-view restaurants built into the arcades of the old city walls. Souvenir sellers, buskers and street entertainers all add to the lively atmosphere. It's easy to while away the hours at café terraces, watching the world go by, or dining alfresco looking across to the twinkling lights of Vila Nova de Gaia. The hub of the waterfront is the **Praça da Ribeira** ❶ (Ribeira Square), overlooked by the Pestana Vintage Porto hotel and packed with riverside cafés. Towards the back of the square is a 1970s fountain with a large bronze, corner-balanced cube, with sculpted pigeons on its sloping sides. Behind it the 18th-century Fonte da Rua de São João (Fountain of St John) was given an update in 2000 with the addition of a modern statue of São João, the patron saint of the city, in the niche. To the west of the square, Rua da Fonte Taurina, one of the oldest streets in the city, is lined by hole-in-the-wall tavernas.

At the eastern end of the Cais da Ribeira, just before the open archway, is a bronze relief commemorating the Ponte Das Barcas tragedy on 29 March 1809, when the pontoon bridge across the river collapsed under the weight of people fleeing from Napoleon's troops. Hundreds of citizens are thought to have drowned, and candles are still lit here in their memory. Through the arch (but not signed) is the **Ascensor da Ribeira** (Ribeira Lift, also known as the Elevador de Lada; Mon–Fri 8am–7pm, shorter hours in winter; free), which whisks you up the steep slope through the ramshackle **Barredo** quarter to Rua de Lada. Alternatively, you can take steps up through this characterful neighbourhood, and on to the Cathedral quarter.

PONTE DOM LUÍS I

Constructed in 1880–86 to link Porto with Vila Nova de Gaia on the south bank of the river, the 172-metre/564ft **Ponte Dom Luís I** ❷ (or Ponte Luís I) was the work of Portuguese engineer Teófilo Seyrig, the former business partner of Gustav Eiffel. The previous bridge was the Ponte Pênsil, and you can still see two granite piers which once supported it. Today's bridge, which forms the backdrop of many a postcard and photo, is a bold, iron, two-tiered structure. Both levels are accessible to pedestrians, the lower also to cars, the upper to the metro. Traffic and trains don't enhance the crossing on foot, but it is well worth going across for the far-reaching views of Porto, Gaia and the **Dona Maria Pia Bridge** (1875–77) upstream, which was designed by Eiffel himself. If you're crossing to Gaia,

The mighty Ponte Dom Luís I

Funicular dos Guindais amid lush vegetation

take the upper tier for the Monastery, the lower one for the port wine lodges.

Still on the Porto side of the river, just beyond the bridge, the **Funicular dos Guindais** (every 10 mins Apr–Oct Mon–Thu & Sun 8am–10pm, Fri and Sat 8am–midnight, Nov–Mar Mon–Thu & Sun 8am–8pm, Fri & Sat 8am–midnight) links the quayside with Batalha in the upper part of the city. A funicular has operated here on and off since 1891. The latest incarnation (2004) is a swish affair which whisks you up (or down) the hillside in a couple of minutes.

CASA DO INFANTE

Ribeira's main monuments lie just inland from the waterfront on the western side. Just north of the Largo do Terreiro is the **Casa do Infante ③** (House of the Prince; Tue–Sun 9.30am–1pm, 2–5.30pm; free at weekends), reputedly the birthplace in 1394 of the Infante Dom Henrique, better known as Henry the Navigator, who launched Portugal's age of discovery. The building is an old customs house, which was created in 1325 and functioned for over 500 years, with a mint also established on-site. The tower was the main royal building in the city and it is believed that João I and his wife Philippa of Lancaster, who were married in Porto, lived here during their long stay in the city. Henry was their fourth and last surviving son. The building today is an Interpretive Centre featuring an exhibition on Henry and the New World, with particular emphasis on the role of Porto. Little remains of the original building, but there are reconstructed sections of the former customs house and mint within the museum, as well as a piece of mosaic flooring from Roman times discovered in the foundations.

Henry the Navigator is omnipresent in this quarter. Cross the Rua Infante Dom Henrique for the eponymous praça (square), dominated by a statue of Henry, high on a pedestal pointing towards the sea. Overlooking the square on the north side is the conspicuous red iron **Mercado Ferreira**

☉ THE FEITORIA INGLESA

Designed by the British Consul John Whitehead and built in 1785–90, the Feitoria Inglesa or English Factory House was created as an exclusive meeting place for British port merchants and financed entirely by their annual contributions. You can't miss the building – a huge neo-Palladian structure on what was previously called the Rua dos Ingleses (Street of the English), where it crosses Rua de São João. From 1811 it became the headquarters of the British Association, set up to promote port and keep traditions alive. Today it is still owned and run by the English port wine companies and hosts traditional social events accompanied, of course, by port (needless to say the collection of vintage ports is priceless). A traditional Wednesday lunch still takes place when members and their guests have blind tastings of vintage port. Decorated with chandeliers, Chippendale furniture, porcelain and silverware, the rooms retain their grandeur. The Feitoria is closed to the public but if you happen to know a member it is well worth a visit.

Tripeiros

Porto was where the fleet for Henry the Navigator's assault on Ceuta in 1415 was fitted out. For this Christian venture against the Moors of North Africa, the people of Porto surrendered the finest cuts of meat in their stores to the navy and lived on tripe instead, thus earning the nickname of *Tripeiros* (literally 'tripe eaters').

Borges, built to replace the old Ribeira market and now home to the **Hard Club,** a huge cultural venue offering a dynamic programme of events at very reasonable prices. It also houses the spacious O Mercado Restaurant/Café, good for tapas and pizzas, with a terrace overlooking the square.

PALÁCIO DA BOLSA

The former stock exchange or **Palácio da Bolsa** ❹ (www.palaciodabolsa.com; Apr–Oct 9am–6.30pm, Nov–Mar 9am–1pm, 2–5.30pm, guided tours only, 30–45 mins), dominating the west side of the square, is evidence of Porto's economic power and prosperity in the late 19th century. It was constructed on the ruins of the ancient convent of São Francisco, which was destroyed by fire, and it remained the city's stock exchange (Bolsa) until the 1990s when it linked up with Lisbon's Bolsa. The desks and benches are long gone, and it has more the feel of a royal residence than a stock exchange. Rooms centre around the glass domed Pátio das Nações, the former trading floor, decorated with the coats of arms of nations which traded with Portugal. The Noble Stairway leads up to grand chambers such as the Court Room, the Golden Room, the Presidents' Room and the General Assembly Room, culminating with the architectural tour de force, the **Arabian Hall**. Replacing the former ballroom and inspired by the Alhambra in Granada, this oval room is adorned with rich Moorish decoration of arabesques and carved woodwork. The room took 18 years to complete and was embellished with 20 kilos of gold leaf. If you happen to be looking for an exotic venue, it's available to rent.

A visit to the Palácio da Bolsa could be combined with wine-sampling in the **Wines of Portugal Tasting Rooms** (Mon–Sat 11am–7pm), inconspicuously set in rooms on the north side of the palace. It's a very relaxed sort of place where you can help yourself to a dozen or so wines at very affordable prices (€1.20–€6.40). There is English labelling for each wine, information on wines from different regions and friendly, helpful staff. The Palácio also has an elegant restaurant, O Comercial, with an affordable set lunch and river views. Just up the hill the **Douro and Port Wine Institute** (free) is the place to learn about port, with an excellent little museum on how port wines are made and (for a small fee) tastings of different varieties.

IGREJA DE SÃO FRANCISCO

Beside the Palácio da Bolsa overlooking the River Douro stands the huge **Igreja de São Francisco** ❺ (daily Mar–May & Oct 9am–7pm, June 9am–7.30pm, July–Sept 9am–8pm, Nov–Feb 9am–6pm). The exterior is simple, grey and Gothic,

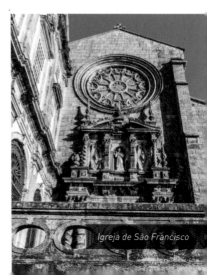

Igreja de São Francisco

built as part of a Franciscan convent in 1383–1425. But the church's interior is like an explosion in a gold factory, swathed from floor to ceiling with a dazzling riot of gilded rococo woodcarving. The 210kg (33 stone) of gold leaf used for the embellishment of the church came from Brazil, Portugal's former colony. The highlight is the gilded and painted altarpiece representing the **Tree of Jesse** (1718–21) on the north wall, depicting Christ's genealogy, the tree rising from the recumbent body of Jesse of Bethlehem, father of King David and culminating in Christ, with Mary and Joseph either side.

The museum displays religious artwork, but of more interest to most visitors are the catacombs. The rich and poor of Porto alike were once buried here, with an estimated 30,000 skulls interred in the cellars. There are numbered panels with dates from 1746–1866 (after which the state banned burials in churches), among them the remains of monks who lived here.

THE SÉ AND AROUND

The Sé or Cathedral is one of the few Romanesque monuments in the city, though much modified since its original construction. It is set high up on the Penaventosa hill and is an unmistakable city landmark. The spacious esplanade, with great views of the old town, tends to attract more crowds than the Sé itself, whose facade is rather austere. It was here that Don

João I married Philippa of Lancaster in 1387 and where Henry the Navigator, their fourth son, was baptised in 1394. The quarter around and below the Sé is the oldest in the city and well worth exploring for its warren of steep alleys and stairways. Steps from here lead all the way down to the Ribeira.

THE SÉ

Built as a Romanesque fortress church with battlements, the **Sé** ❻ (daily Apr–Oct 9am–12.30pm, 2.30–7pm, Nov–Mar until 6pm; free; Cloister daily Apr–Oct 9am–12.15pm, 2.30–6.30pm, Nov–Mar Mon–Sat 9am–12.15pm, 2.30–5.30pm; charge) presents a medley of styles, from Romanesque through Gothic to Baroque. As you enter the church the eye is inevitably drawn to the monumental altar flanked by barley twist columns and

Porto's Sé and pillory

a riot of gilt carving with saints and angels. This was the work of Nasoni (see page 47), who in his flamboyant style also decorated the walls of the chancel, embellished the chapels and added the loggia on the north side. In the left transept the Chapel of the Holy Sacrament is known for its silver retable, executed by local silversmiths in the 17th century in Mannerist style.

Close to the cathedral portal is the entrance to the Cistercian **Cloister**, with a double tier of slim Corinthian capitals supporting Gothic arches. The sober granite is relieved by seven panels of decorative *azulejos* (tiles) depicting scenes from Solomon's *Song of Songs*. A stairway designed by Nasoni leads to the upper storey with 18th-century *azulejos* showing rural and mythological scenes. The adjoining Sala Capitular (Chapter Room) has yet more *azulejos*, this time showing hunting scenes. Steps then take you down to the Treasury, which displays lavish gold and silver vestments and reliquaries.

TERREIRO DA SÉ

The spacious square in front of the church, the **Terreiro da Sé ❼**, has a Manueline-style pillory, complete with hooks where criminals were hanged. This is a replica, erected here in 1945, but gives you an idea of the harsh penalties of former times. On the north side of the church is an equestrian statue of a very upright Vímara Peres, vassal of Afonso III of Léon, Count of Portugal, who captured ancient Portucale from the Moors in AD 868. The portico on this side of the church is decorated with fine 18th-century blue and white *azulejos* (tiles).

The reconstructed medieval tower just below the esplanade houses one of the city's main tourist offices – with very helpful staff.

PAÇO EPISCOPAL

Abutting the cathedral on the south side of the square is the monumental **Paço Episcopal** ❽ (Bishop's Palace; Mon, Tue, Thu–Sat 9am–1pm, 2–6pm; guided tours every half hour), former residence of the bishops of Porto. It was built on the foundation of a former castle, but was largely reconstructed by Nasoni in the 18th century. The palace has been host to diverse historical events

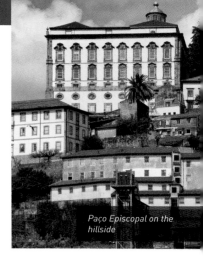

Paço Episcopal on the hillside

including the coronation of the first King of Portugal, as well as serving as a fortress – occupied by the Liberalists – during the Portuguese Civil War, when it was put under siege. It later played a similar role for troops of Sir Arthur Wellesley (later Duke of Wellington) during the Peninsular War. After the fall of the monarchy this was Porto's city hall and was opened to the public by request under the will of the last bishop.

The palace is a familiar landmark in the city, its four-storey riverside facade one of the most prominent buildings on the hill above Ribeira. A tour of the rooms can be quite heavy-going, particularly the portraits of all the bishops in the Audience Room, but there are lovely views of the city and river from the terraces. The architectural highlight is Nasoni's magnificent Baroque main staircase with rococo decorative features. The colourfully decorated glass dome lights the whole of the entrance vestibule and stairway.

Casa-Museu Guerra Junqueiro

CASA-MUSEU GUERRA JUNQUEIRO

Behind the Sé lies the **Casa-Museu Guerra Junqueiro** ❾ (Tue–Sun 10am–12.30pm, 2–5.30pm; free at weekends), a handsome Baroque mansion hidden away on the charming Rua de Dom Hugo. This was the last home of poet Guerra Junqueiro (1850–1923), who was also a politician, viticulturist, scientist, philosopher and art collector. His works of art are displayed throughout the house much as they might have been during his lifetime. The collection consists of decorative arts from the 15th to 19th centuries, including elaborate furniture, fine silver and sculptures, both from Iberia and far-flung corners of the Portuguese empire. A new modern section of the museum hosts temporary exhibitions and there is now a café with outdoor tables overlooking the quiet garden with its statue of the seated poet.

Continue along the Rua Dom Hugo for the restored and remodelled 17th-century Capela de Nossa Senhora das

Verdades (Tue–Sun 10am–5.30pm, brief closing at lunchtime), a pretty chapel which reopened in 2018 and serves as a welcome centre for pilgrims on their way to Santiago de Compostela. Just beyond it a steep stairway, carved through the remaining sections of the medieval town walls, leads down through the tangle of steep medieval alleys and stairways of the **Barredo** working class quarter and on to the waterfront.

IGREJA DE SANTA CLARA

Tucked away on a pretty shaded square, east of the Sé, is the **Igreja de Santa Clara** ❿ (Largo de 1 Dezembro; Mon–Fri 10am–12.30pm, 2.30–5pm, Sat 10am–12.30pm). The squat facade of this inconspicuous church belies a treasure trove of Baroque detail inside. The church is of Gothic origin but, like so many churches in Porto, underwent major modifications in the 17th and 18th centuries. The interior is amazingly lavish, encrusted with gilded Baroque and rococo woodwork (talhas douradas). Almost every inch is covered in gold leaf. It is a wonderful site at any time of day but spectacular when the sun pours in through the windows of the nave. The only unadorned side is the big grill at the back of the church, behind which nuns from the convent participated in services. The beautiful choir area leading to the convent is currently undergoing a meticulous renovation and is closed to the public. Sadly the convent cloisters are also out of bounds, being part of the neighbouring police station.

The church stands next to one of the best preserved parts of the 14th-century city wall, the **Muralha Fernandina**, named after King Fernando I. These granite walls at one time surrounded the entire city.

BAIXA (DOWNTOWN)

The city, which began down by the river, has expanded considerably beyond the old walls. The Praça da Liberdade (Freedom Square), at the southern end of the broad Avenida dos Aliados, is regarded as the true heart of the city. To the east of Aliados (as it is commonly called) are the principal shopping streets and the centuries-old Bolhão market (currently closed for restoration). The area to the west has undergone a rebirth in the last few years and the quarter around Rua Galeria de Paris and Rua Cândido dos Reis, known jointly as 'the galleries of Paris', positively buzzes with nightclubs, jazz venues and late-night bars. The nearby Clérigos complex is the main cultural attraction of the Baixa and its lofty tower is a Baroque beacon visible from almost the entire city.

AVENIDA DOS ALIADOS

Atypical of Porto, the Avenida dos Aliados is a showcase of early 20th-century Beaux-Arts and neoclassical grandeur. Buildings topped with domes, spires or statues are home to banks, insurance offices and hotels. At the northern end stands the dominant Câmara Municipal (Town Hall), with the neighbouring main tourist office at 25, Rua Clube dos Fenianos. The boulevard slopes down to the **Praça da Liberdade** ⓫, a stage for celebrations, festivities, music, merrymaking, mourning and rebellion. At its centre is an equestrian statue of Pedro IV (1798–1834), founder and first ruler of Brazil, who was nicknamed 'The Liberator'. Overlooking the square on the south side, the 5-star Intercontinental Hotel occupies the majestic Palácio das Cardosas. A monastery once stood here but it fell into disrepair, being converted into a private palace in the 19th century. The purchase came with the condition that the building would have the same facade that the monks had planned for the reconstruction of the monastery – hence the huge neoclassical facade. Step inside and it's anything but monastic: all marble, chandeliers and grandeur.

ESTAÇÃO DE SÃO BENTO

Just east of the square is the airy and ornate **Estação de São Bento** ⑫, far too handsome to be a railway hub. Named after the Benedictine monastery which originally occupied the site, the station was designed by architect José Marquês da Silva and opened in 1916 in the French Beaux-Arts style. Its great entrance hall is decorated with wonderful blue and white *azulejo* panels executed by Jorge Colaço in 1905–16. The tiles number around 20,000 and depict key historical events in Portugal's

Estação de São Bento is stunning and covered in azulejos

history and scenes of traditional life in northern Portugal. For anyone arriving by train it's a wonderful welcome to the city.

PRAÇA DA BATALHA

Just up Rua 31 de Janeiro from the railway station is the **Praça da Batalha** with the **Teatro Nacional São João** ⓲ (www.tnsj.pt; guided tours Tue–Sat at 12.30pm; free for children under 10), the city's main theatre and opera venue. Built to replace the late 18th-century theatre which was destroyed

⊘ A FEAST FOR THE EYES

Apart from one or two captions, some too high to read, there is no information at São Bento station's on its hall of *azulejos* – perhaps not surprisingly given this is a station not an art gallery. So, in brief: the dramatic upper panel on the left-hand wall is a scene from the Battle of Arcos de Valdevez, considered Portugal's first War of Independence (1140), when knights led by Afonso I of Portugal fought and defeated troops led by Alfonso VII, King of León. The lower panel shows Egas Moniz offering himself and his wife and sons to the King of León for execution in order to save the besieged town from occupation. The upper panel of the far right-hand wall illustrates the celebratory entrance into Porto in 1387 of King João I of Portugal with his English bride Philippa of Lancaster, daughter of John of Gaunt, thus sealing the long-standing alliance between Portugal and England. The lower panel shows the conquest of the Moors at Ceuta in 1415 led by Henry the Navigator. Other more tranquil scenes portray workers in the vineyards, at the watermill, and, opposite the entrance, Our Lady of the Remedies performing miracles at the holy fountain in the town of Lamego.

by fire, it was designed by architect Marquês da Silva and inspired by the Palais Garnier opera house in Paris. Theatrical productions are usually in Portuguese, but there are tours in English of the splendid auditorium, as well as the rehearsal and dressing rooms. Conspicuous for its lofty setting above the square is the Baroque **Igreja de São Ildefonso** (Mon–Sat 9am–noon, 3–6.30pm, Sun 9am–1pm, 6–8pm). The highlight is the facade, with 11,000 blue and white *azulejos* depicting scenes from the life of the church's patron saint. The tiles, only added in the early 1930s, were the work of Jorge Colaço, the same artist who embellished São Bento station.

Azulejo-clad Igreja de São Ildefonso

RUA DE SANTA CATARINA

Running north from the Igreja de São Ildefonso is the mainly pedestrianised **Rua de Santa Caterina**, the principal shopping street for both locals and tourists. Even for non-shoppers it's an attractive street for a stroll, with mosaic-patterned pavements and a variety of facades from striking Art Nouveau, especially at the lower end, to the flamboyant pink pipes of the Via Catarina shopping mall. Tourists normally make a beeline for the famous **Café Majestic** ⓮ (see page 111) at No. 112, which has been serving coffee since 1921. Originally called the 'Elite', it was known in its earlier life as a place of political and cultural gatherings. Today it caters almost entirely to tourist and prices are sky high for Porto, but you won't find a more elegant café setting in the city. Further up the street and quite unexpected is the lovely **Capela de Santa Catarina** (confusingly also called the Capela das Almas), completely clad in blue and white *azulejos*. The tiles depict scenes from the life of St Francis of Assisi and St Catherine. As is normal with churches in Porto, the tiles came much later than the church, in this case in 1929, over 130 years after the building was constructed. This is a popular little church and if you visit during Mass, the pews will be packed.

MERCADO DO BOLHÃO

Just west of the Rua de Santa Catarina, the famous **Mercado do Bolhão ⑮**, one of the most iconic buildings in Porto, recently closed down for a complete overhaul. The site has hosted a market since 1838 when the city council built a square on a meadow crossed by a stream (the name Bolhão means 'big bubble'). The present two-tiered wrought-iron hall was not built until 1914. For years this has been the belly of the city, with loud earthy characters behind huge piles of fruit and vegetables, and stalls selling live rabbits, tripe, pigs' trotters and all manner of sausages and cheeses. The building has been deteriorating for some time, leading to its closure in 2018 for at least two years. Given the latest proposals to use the upper level for shops and restaurants, it is unlikely to retain its traditional character.

The area, however, is still a good one for food, with the market stalls temporarily located in La Vie shopping centre, nearby on Rua Fernandes Tomás, and plenty of gourmet temptations around the market square. The A Pérola do Bolão, which has an instagrammable Art Nouveau facade on Rua Formosa, is packed with spicy sausages, mountain cheeses, nuts and port wine. On the same street, opposite the market, the Confeitaria do Bolão has been serving home-made bread and pastries since 1896. They also offer a very affordable daily set menu (€7.40, including a glass of wine).

THE CLÉRIGOS COMPLEX

West of Praça da Liberdade, the Rua dos Clérigos leads up to the Clérigos Church with its exuberant facade. The

Bigger fish to fry at Mercado do Bolão

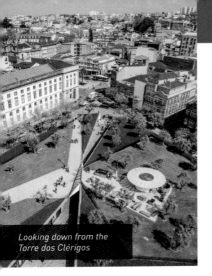

Looking down from the Torre dos Clérigos

Brotherhood of the Clerics (Clérigos), founded in 1707, was a merger of three different brotherhoods in Porto, but all with the same mission – to help members of the clergy in sickness, poverty and death. In 1732–9 the Church of Clérigos was designed by Nicolau Nasoni, the Italian-born architect and painter (see page 47). The brotherhood moved here in 1748. The 75-metre (246ft)

Torre dos Clérigos ⓰ (www.torredosclerigos.pt; daily 9am–7pm; combined ticket available online for church, tower and museum; church only is free), also by Nasoni, was built in 1753 as a landmark for ships coming up the Douro. A climb up the 225 steps is rewarded with a 360 degree panorama of the city (be prepared for queues). Exhibitions and viewing platforms en route allow you to catch your breath and plaques help you to spot city landmarks and compare the height of other 'skyscrapers in the world'. Two sections are devoted to Nasoni.

The entire complex underwent major restoration in 2014 and visitors now pass from the tower to a new museum on the Brotherhood of the Clerics and then to the renovated Upper Choir. This opens up dramatic views onto the beautiful Baroque **Igreja dos Clérigos**, distinguished by its elliptical nave and altarpiece. It was Nasoni's dying wish to be buried here, but no one knows exactly where, or even if he did end up here. Tests are currently being carried out on skeletons discovered during renovations in the hope of solving the mystery.

In the lee of the tower is the **Passeio dos Clérigos**, a small modern shopping mall and, more appealing, its rooftop landscaped garden with a chic alfresco bar for coffee, cocktails and lounging on comfy cushions. The olive trees planted here came from the Algarve. Just to the west is the **Jardim da Cordoaria**, in Campo dos Mártires da Pátria, named after the ropemakers

⊘ NICOLAU NASONI

Nicolau Nasoni was an Italian artist and architect born in Tuscany in 1691. He first worked as an apprentice in Siena before leaving for Malta in 1722, where he painted frescoes in Valletta's cathedral and embellished grand buildings for the Order of the Knights of St John. Porto was thriving in the 1920s and Nasoni moved here in 1925, making it his home. The Portuguese loved his flair for theatrics and he became one of the most influential figures in Portuguese Baroque and rococo architecture, creating, remodelling or enhancing churches and palaces. Nasoni's speciality was an architectural form called *talha dourada* – carved woodwork decorated with gold leaf, producing a flamboyant and opulent effect. He renovated and redecorated Porto's cathedral but his real tour de force was the Clérigos complex (see page 45), which he worked on for over three decades. The prolific architect's work took him beyond Porto and included the Mateus Palace, familiar from the labels on bottles of Mateus Rosé. His final request was to be buried in the Clérigos church, but no one knows where his body rests. Researchers are currently testing skeletal remains to see if his dying wish was honoured.

(cordoaria) who once worked here. Today it's popular with students from the neighbouring university building. The most eye-catching features here are the four pieces – *Thirteen Laughing at Each Other* – by Spanish sculptor Juan Muñoz, installed in 2001 when Porto was European Capital of Culture.

LIVRARIA LELLO

A short stroll up the Rua das Carmelitas brings you to the neo-Gothic facade of the Livraria Chardron, better known as the **Livraria Lello** ⑰ (www.livrarialello.pt; Mon–Fri 10am–7.30pm, Sat 10am–7pm). It's so popular that you have to either book online or purchase a voucher (redeemable against the purchase of books) at the corner shop up the road, where there is invariably a queue. It may seem strange for a bookshop to have an admission fee, but the system was introduced a few years ago when the shop was facing a crisis in the growth of visitor numbers. It's not just the stunning Art Nouveau interior with its dramatic double red staircase and opulent ceiling, nor the wonderful collection of books, old and new, that draw the long queues of punters. It's also the fact that the shop was frequented by *Harry Potter* author J.K. Rowling when she lived and worked as a teacher in Porto in the 1990s (she was married briefly to a Portuguese man) and the bookstore with its staircase may well have been the inspiration for scenes in Hogwarts.

If you spot young Portuguese in black capes in the city, they are not *Harry Potter* fans but students of Porto University. You may see them coming and going from the huge rectangular university building overlooking the nearby **Praça de Gomes Teixeira** ⑱, with its palms and lion fountain. The Café D'Ouro on the far side dates back to 1909 and, confusingly, is universally known as **Café Piolho**. A meeting place for students and teachers from the university, it is one of most famous cafés in Porto. The two nearby Baroque churches, **Igreja das Carmelitas** and **Igreja do Carmo**, appear at first glance to stand side by side, but look closer and you can see they are separated by a very narrow structure – the thinnest house in Porto. This was built to comply with an unwritten law forbidding two churches sharing a common wall, and in this case perhaps ensuring no amorous links between the nuns of the Carmelite Church and the monks of the Carmo church. The east wall of the latter is decorated by striking blue and white *azulejos*, depicting the legendary founding of the Carmelite order on Mount Carmel.

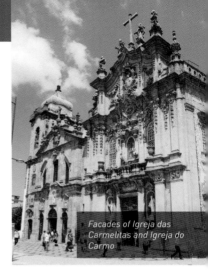
Facades of Igreja das Carmelitas and Igreja do Carmo

CENTRO PORTUGUÊS DE FOTOGRAFIA

A stone's throw south of the Clérigos complex, the vast neoclassical building on Largo Amor de Perdição is home to the **Centro Português de Fotografia** ⑲ (Portuguese Centre for Photography; www.cpf.pt; Mar–June and Sept–Oct Tue–Fri 10am–6pm, Sat and Sun 3–7pm, July–Aug daily 10am–6pm, Nov–Feb Tue–Fri 10am–12.30pm, 2–5pm, Sat and Sun 3–7pm; free). An ex-prison, it was built in 1767 and housed inmates on three floors: the dark, dank and chilly ground-floor dungeons;

the second-floor, which was slightly more salubrious and included cells for women; and the third floor with individual prison cells for 'people with status', which were only locked at night. One of the cells belonged to the famous 19th-century novelist, Camilo Castelo Branco, who was locked up here for adultery. A bronze statue in the square outside shows him embracing his naked lover.

The prison was closed in 1974, soon after the Revolution. The building today hosts temporary exhibitions and on the top floor a permanent and rare collection of cameras of every description, including 19th-century studio cameras used to take pictures for the identification of prisoners and spy cameras from the 60s–80s, disguised as Pepsi cans or Camel cigarette packets.

The stark Centro Português de Fotografia

The area to the south was the centre of the medieval **Jewish quarter**. Stroll down the Rua de São Bento da Vitória with the eponymous monastery on the right (guided tours Mon–Fri at noon), built in the 17th and 18th centuries by Benedictine monks and preserving a beautiful cloister. The road brings you down to the Church of Nossa Senhora da Vitória and the **Miradouro da Vitória ㉔**, with splendid views of the city and Vila Nova de Gaia across the river. It's a favourite spot at sunset.

RUA DAS FLORES

To the east, and linking the town centre with Ribeira, is the delightful **Rua das Flores**, or Street of Flowers. The name dates back to the 16th century when this was an area of gardens belonging to the bishop of Porto. It was favoured by the nobles and bourgeoisie, who built their luxury mansions here. In the 19th century the street was the haunt of the literati and in 1855 a poetry journal was founded here by the 'Poets of the Flores Street Movement'. Only a decade ago it was off the tourist track: dark and traffic-ridden, with buildings in a state of disrepair. Now pedestrianised and flanked by handsome mansions, seductive shops and cafés, it is a top spot in the city for a leisurely stroll.

At the far end, just before the Largo de São Domingos, you're unlikely to miss the elaborate Baroque facade of the Igreja da Misericórdia by Nicolau Nasoni. Entrance is only possible via the adjoining **Museu da Igreja Misericórdia ㉑** (www.mmipo.pt; daily Oct–Mar 10am–5.30pm, Apr–Sept 10am–6.30pm; guided tours available). Until 2013 the building was home to the Santa Casa da Misericórdia, founded in 1499 as a charitable institution providing health care and assisting impoverished prisoners. In 2014 the building underwent a complete transformation and it is now a surprisingly interesting museum. Visits start on the top floor, with a collection of fascinating medical

equipment used for brain surgery, electric shock therapy, blood-letting and other largely defunct medical procedures. The range of exhibits and memorabilia gives a real insight into the breadth of the organisation and the help that it gave; its importance to the community is also evidenced by the gallery of solemn portraits of its benefactors. The next floor down displays a range of painting and sculpture from the 16th to the 18th centuries, and a room of religious artefacts collected by the Misericórdia, including 16th to 18th-century gold and silverware, vestments and tiny crucifixes. The star work of art is on the first floor: the beautiful, enigmatic and anonymous painting, *Fons Vitae* or *The Fountain of Life* (*c*.1520), portraying King Manuel, his wife and his two children on their knees, facing the crucified Christ. Visits end with views down into the Misericórdia church.

MIRAGAIA AND MASSARELOS

The quarters of Miragaia and Massarelos lie west of the city centre, both bordering the River Douro. Miragaia is one of the most picturesque neighbourhoods of Porto, with its cobbled alleys and jumble of pastel-washed or tiled houses climbing up the steep slopes. At its eastern end it blends seamlessly with neighbouring Ribeira, but has noticeably fewer tourists. The quarter dates back to medieval days when it was outside the city walls, and hence home to Jews and Armenians. Massarelos, stretching west to the Arrábida Bridge and north up the hillsides towards Boavista, is a larger and more varied quarter. Many of its grander former residences now form part of the university. The main focus for tourists is the **Jardim do Palácio de Cristal**, whose romantic gardens climb the steep slopes and afford glorious river views.

RIVERSIDE MIRAGAIA

Miragaia used to be a quarter of fishermen and the **Igreja de São Pedro de Miragaia** (Tue–Sat 3.30–7pm, Sun 10am–11.30am; free) is dedicated to St Peter, patron saint of fishermen. The original medieval church was demolished to make way for this Baroque building and the blue and white *azulejos* (tiles) embellishing its facade were added in 1863–76. Inside are gilded wood carvings and, unusually, a 16th-century Flemish Pentecost triptych in the Confraria Museum. (If locked, ask the custodian for access.)

Miragaia means 'Looking at Gaia', and the views across the river are one of its main attractions. However, some of the best views from lower Miragaia were obliterated by the monumental neoclassical **Alfândega Nova** ㉒ (New Customs House), built on the waterfront in 1860–80. Although essential to Porto's burgeoning commerce, this also wiped out the ancient fisherman's beach and a shipyard. The building lost its role when the port moved to Leixões in Matosinhos. Today's building, renovated and extended, is somewhat daunting, geared more to conventions, exhibitions and training programmes than to visiting tourists. It is home to the **Museu dos Transportes e Comunicações** (Museum of Transport and Communications; www.amtc.pt; Tue–Fri 10am–1pm, 2–6pm,

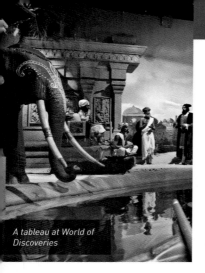

A tableau at World of Discoveries

Sat and Sun 3–7pm, last entry one hour before closing; Customs House Museum is free), accessed at the back of the building. Head up to the first floor for *The Engine of the Republic*, a display of cars which have served Portugal's presidents since the creation of the Republic in 1910, starting with a horse-drawn carriage. *Comunicar*, on the same floor, is a lively multimedia exhibition on the many forms of manmade communication. On the second-floor, the rarely visited antiquated *Customs House Museum* has no English information apart from a video on the history of the building.

If you have children in tow, they are more likely to be enthralled by the **World of Discoveries** (www.worldofdiscoveries.com; Mon–Sat 10am–6pm, Sat and Sun 10am–7pm, last entry half hour before closing) behind the Alfândega Nova, a theme park and interactive museum on Portugal's history. It's all good fun and an easy way for youngsters to learn about the great Portuguese explorers, the exotic lands they discovered and the caravels they sailed in. The grand finale is the Disney-style boat trip, with audio guides, through 'the New Worlds'.

MUSEU NACIONAL DE SOARES DOS REIS

The northern section of Miragaia is home to one of Porto's largest and most imposing palaces, now housing the **Museu**

Nacional de Soares dos Reis  (Rua de Dom Manuel ll 44; www.museusoaresdosreis.gov.pt; Tue–Sun 10am–6pm), the main art gallery of Porto. The neoclassical Carrancas palace was once home to the Jewish family of Moraes e Castro, nicknamed Carranca, who operated a flourishing gold and silver workshop here. The French General and Statesman, Marshal Soult, lived here for six weeks in 1809 during the Peninsular War, before being driven out by troops under the command of Arthur Wellesley (the future Duke of Wellington). The palace has also been the abode of royalty. Founded in 1933, the museum was created as a repository for works of art taken from convents that had been abandoned or abolished during the Portuguese Civil War. The four-sided palace centres around a delightful courtyard and a garden of camellia trees, with *azulejos* and a garden-view café.

The permanent collection starts on the second floor with the decorative arts: fine porcelain, silver, glass and furnishings. Highlights include a large tapestry depicting the return of Vasco da Gama from the east and some small French and Flemish paintings, among them a keenly observed portrait of a woman by Clouet, the 16th-century court painter of Henry II of France. The more modern galleries

Museu Nacional de Soares dos Reis

on the first floor display paintings from the 19th to the 20th centuries, notable among them the landscapes of Silva Porto and the Impressionist-style paintings of Italy and Portugal by Henrique Pousão, who died in 1884 at the age of 25.

But the real highlight of the museum is the gallery devoted to works by the 19th-century sculptor António Soares dos Reis (1847–89). Born in 1847 in Vila Nova da Gaia – which was also where he committed suicide at the age of 41 – he was greatly influenced by his stays in Paris and Rome, where he learned to work with Carrara marble, famously used by Michelangelo. Although largely unrecognised during his lifetime, he was prolific and versatile, producing works in plaster, bronze and marble, portraying historical, allegorical and contemporary figures. Particularly moving are the *Bust of the Negro Boy*, *Youth*

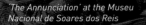

'The Annunciation' at the Museu Nacional de Soares dos Reis

with the Hammer and what is widely held as his finest work, the classical *O Desterrado* (The Exile), executed when he was only 24. There are also realistic busts of contemporaries and grandees.

THE ARTS BLOCK

Defining the northern border of Miragaia is the **Rua de Miguel Bombarda**, a haven for arty shoppers with its hip galleries, concept stores, vintage and design boutiques. Every two months the galleries simultaneously hold exhibitions by national and international artists, normally on a Saturday from 4–5pm. Entry to the galleries is free. At Rua Miguel Bombarda 285 is the misleadingly named **Centro Comercial Bombarda** ㉔ (CCB; Mon–Sat noon–8pm), a small sleek mall and creative hub of independent Portuguese boutiques and galleries. Novelty is the byword here: a stucco ear perhaps, a papier mâché head (and you can watch them being made), a knitted bow tie, organic cosmetics, vintage accessories, cool jewellery and a sustainable mini-farm selling organic goods. If you're visiting the quarter, note that the opening hours are normally Monday to Saturday from noon until 8pm.

JARDIM DO PALÁCIO DE CRISTAL

Bordering Miragaia in Massarelos is the 8-hectare (20-acre) **Jardim do Palácio de Cristal** ㉕ (main entrance Rua Dom Manuel II; Tue–Sat 10am–12.30pm and 2–5.30pm, Sun 2–5.30pm; free at weekends), full of romantic gardens with terraces on a steep hill and some of the best river views in the city. From the south side you can even spot the Atlantic rollers at Foz do Douro. A natural magnet for city-dwellers, this green lung of the city has exotic trees and plants, themed gardens, fountains, ponds and statues – not to mention the strutting peacocks and noisy cockerels who roam freely in this leafy haven.

The garden was originally designed in the 19th century by German landscape architect Émille David. The **Palácio de Cristal** (daily Apr–Sept 8am–9pm, Oct–Mar 8am–7pm; free), a mushroom-like domed sports arena, was built in 1951 for the World Hockey Championships. It replaced a rather more elegant iron and glass palace, similar to London's Crystal Palace, dating from the 1860s. The building is also called the Pavilhão Rosa Mota, after the Portuguese Olympic marathon champion. With a seating capacity of 10,000, the pavilion holds concerts and sporting events and is one of Porto's leading entertainment venues.

Geometric landscaping at the Jardim do Palácio de Cristal

Set in the green splendour of the gardens to the west is the newly restored **Museu Romântico** ㉖ (Tue–Sat 10am–5pm, Sun 10am–noon, 2–5pm; free at weekends). The house was bought in the early 19th century by a port wine millionaire, Antonio Ferreira Pinto Basto, but it's main claim to fame is as the last home of Carlos Alberto, the King of Piedmont and Sardinia – albeit that he was here for only a couple of months before dying in 1849. The previous year he had led one of the Liberation movements in the Unification of Italy, but was defeated by the Austrians in the Battle of Novar in 1849 and abdicated in favour of his eldest son, Victor Emmanuel, before fleeing to Portugal. Pinto Basto offered him refuge in his mansion in Porto. The house was bought by the state in the mid-20th century and opened as the Museum of Quinta da Macieirinha in 1972. It is laid out more or less as it would have been in the king's day, with his works of art and furniture, some original, some reproductions. A visit includes various salons, the oratory where the king attended mass daily, the Ball Room and the King's Hall where he received visitors and where his body lay in state.

Next to the museum is the Antiqvvm Restaurant (see page 111), tempting for its views of the river and its Michelin-starred cuisine. But beware that deep pockets are definitely required – and you probably need to book in advance.

Steps from the museum lead all the way down to the river-front, passing the Baroque **Igreja de Massarelos** en route, with its bell towers and tiled facade. The church was built on the site of a ruined chapel founded in 1394 by the Brotherhood of the Amas do Corpo Santo, a group of navigators who had survived a storm when returning from England. The brotherhood was dedicated to the protection of seafarers and merchants and it is rumoured that Henry the Navigator was a member.

ALONG THE WATERFRONT

On the riverfront going west is the **Museu do Carro Eléctrico** ㉗ (Tram Museum; www.museudocarroelectrico.pt; Mon–6pm, Tue–Sun 10am–6pm), which charts the evolution of the tram network in Porto. Better still, you can actually hop on an operational vintage tram; both No. 18 and No. 1 stop here – the No. 1 is particularly scenic, running beside the river from central Porto to Foz do Douro on the coast. The large letters on the museum building, STCP, stand for the Sociedade de Transportes Coletivos do Porto. The organisation resurrected a couple of tram routes in the city and opened a museum in 1992 in the Massarelos thermoelectric power plant, which fed the network for the first 45 years. The century-old machines have been restored and are now on view in the new Machinery Hall.

Museu do Carro Eléctrico

The trams on display span over 100 years, from an early horse-drawn tram-car to a special tram for smokers (the *fumista*), tramcars for the transport of fish and familiar models of the late 20th century.

Scenes westwards to the Atlantic are framed by the vast concrete swoop of the **Ponte da Arrábida** ㉘, spanning the River Douro. When it opened in 1963 this was the longest concrete arch in the world. There is no pedestrian access across, but should you wish to climb the bridge check out www.portobridgeclimb.com.

> ### The Porto Card
>
> The Porto Card includes free admission or reduced fees to museums and tourist attractions, plus an optional travel card for unlimited access to metro, buses and urban trains. Cards are available online (www.visitportoandnorth. travel) and at tourist offices. A card without transport costs €6, €10, €13 and €15 for 1, 2, 3 and 4 days; passes with travel for the same periods are €13, €20, €25 and €33.

BOAVISTA AND SERRALVES

Northwest of the city centre, Boavista is an upmarket modern suburb of luxury hotels, designer stores, villas and one of the city's top sights: the Casa da Música or 'House of Music'. The Avenida da Boavista slices through suburbia and stretches westwards all the way to the Atlantic coast at Foz do Douro. At the Porto end is the huge roundabout, Praça Mouzinho de Albuquerque, more familiarly known as the Rotunda da Boavista, with a central garden, the Jardim da Boavista. The column at its centre, the Monumento aos Heróis da Guerra Peninsular, commemorates the defeat of the French in the

Peninsular War (1807–14). The lion, symbolising the alliance between the Portuguese and British, is bringing down the Imperial Eagle, carried into battle by the Grande Armée of Napoleon.

Between Boavista and the coast is the outstanding Serralves Museum of Contemporary Art and its beautiful park.

CASA DA MÚSICA

On the northwest side of the Rotunda da Boavista, you are unlikely to miss the space-age **Casa da Música** ㉙ (www.casadamusica.com; guided tours in Portuguese and English at 11am and 4pm), an exuberant, avant-garde concert hall designed by Dutch architect (and Star Wars fan) Rem Koolhaas. It was conceived to mark Porto's year as European Capital of Culture in 2001, but was not in fact completed until 2005. Since then it has been drawing large numbers of music fans of all persuasions. Concerts range from pop to Baroque, with DJs some nights and the occasional free (or very cheap) event. The main auditorium seats around 1,300 and, unusually, is lit with natural daylight through two walls made entirely of glass. A second auditorium accommodates 300 seated and 600 standing. These can be seen on informative hour-long guided tours which include other areas of the seventh-floor building, such as the VIP hall and rooftop terrace with fine views. The top-floor Casa da Música Restaurant (Mon–Sat for lunch and dinner) has good-value set menus.

MARKET, CEMETERY AND SYNAGOGUE

To the south of the Boavista Rotunda (and technically in Massarelos) is the renovated **Mercado de Bom Sucesso** (Praça Bom Sucesso 3; Sun–Thu 10am–11pm, Fri and Sat

The arresting Casa da Música

10am–midnight, fresh produce Mon–Sat 9am–8pm), which lives up to its name: a whole range of beautifully presented gourmet treats under one stylish roof. Along with fresh produce for sale, there are 44 outlets for quick and tasty meals or tapas, including delis with delicious hams and suckling pig and seafood stalls with squid and ceviche. Just take your pick and choose a table. Heaters will keep you warm in the winter months. Within the same complex is the 4-star designer Hotel da Música where, as you probably guessed, music is the theme.

To the west is the **Cemitério de Agramonte** (Rua de Agramonte; daily 8.30am–5pm; free), looking a little out of place in the largely modern surrounds. Built in 1855 for the corpses from an epidemic of the plague, the cemetery was later expanded to accommodate those of Porto's literati and well-to-do. A fine collection of sculpture includes works by Soares dos Reis (see page 54 for the Museu Nacional Soares

Fundação Serralves knows a trick or two

dos Reis) and António Teixeira Lopes. If the cemetery is shut you can peek through the railings at some of the incredibly elaborate mausoleums.

On the far side of the cemetery, accessed from the Rua Guerra Junqueiro, is the striking Art Deco **Sinagoge Kadoorie** (www.comunidade-israelita-porto.org), the largest synagogue in the Iberian peninsula. For security reasons visits and tours are by appointment only (email: tourism@comunidade-israelita-porta.org). A guided visit gives a fascinating history of the synagogue, its founder and the story of Jews in Portugal and Spain over 500 years.

FUNDAÇÃO SERRALVES

Between Boavista and the coast lies an outstanding cultural complex, the **Fundação Serralves** (Rua Dom João de Castro 210; 3.5km/2.2 miles from Jardim Boavista, 6km/3.7 miles west of the city centre; www.serralves.pt; Mon–Fri 10am–7pm, Sat and Sun 10am–6pm; combined ticket for Museum, Villa and Park, or half-price for Park only; whole complex free on first Sun of month). From Casa da Música metro station you can take buses 201, 203, 502 or 504.

The complex is most famously home to the **Museu de Arte Contemporânea ⑳** (Museum of Contemporary Art), the most influential contemporary art museum in Portugal. Integrated seamlessly into the surrounding landscape, the three-storey museum is the work of Álvaro Siza Vieira, born in 1933 in Matosinhos, winner in 1992 of the prestigious Pritzker Prize and one of the world's finest architects – though little known in Britain. The 14 exhibition halls are all awash with light, and the works of art are wonderfully arranged on vivid white walls. The museum has over 4,500 works, around 1,700 owned by the Foundation, the remaining from private and public collections. The focus is on contemporary art from the 1960s to the present day and regularly changing exhibitions of leading local and international artists. Serralves is also a venue for concerts, dance and other events, including the annual art-themed Serralves em Festa, which takes place in May or June. The complex has an auditorium, an art bookshop, a gift shop full of creative Portuguese designer gifts, a garden-view restaurant with a good buffet lunch and a *casa de chà* (tea house) in the park.

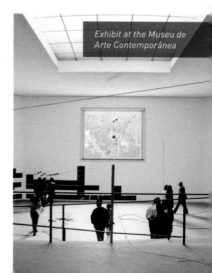

Exhibit at the Museu de Arte Contemporânea

The museum is set in the magnificent 18-hectare (44.5-acre) **Serralves Park**, which comprises harmoniously linked gardens, treelined paths, woodlands, a lake and a traditional farm. Dotted around the park are sculptures and other works of art from the Serralves collection, including a whopping and very photogenic red trowel by Claes Oldenburg. A key feature is the **Casa de Serralves**, a beautiful pink Art Deco villa from the 1930s, originally designed as a private residence by the second Count of Vizela, Carlos Alberto Cabral. The villa, which occasionally showcases temporary exhibitions, looks stunning against the greenery and is particularly impressive if approached via the fountains.

VILA NOVA DE GAIA

No trip to Porto is complete without a visit to the cellars of at least one of the port wine lodges where the city's most famous export is stored and aged. These are all located at Vila Nova de Gaia (or just 'Gaia'), across the River Douro and techni-

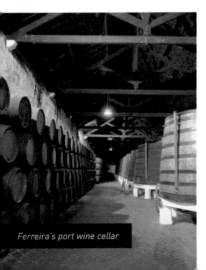

Ferreira's port wine cellar

cally a separate city from Porto. The port is actually produced 60 miles (97km) inland in the Upper Douro region, where vines are grown on the steep stone terraces. Here the blisteringly hot summers and freezing winters create a unique microclimate that produces intensely flavourful grapes. But it's Porto, with its mild and humid climate, that provides the ideal conditions for storing the wines, and every spring the young ports are brought down from river-hugging *quintas* (estates) to the cellars in Vila Gaia de Nova. Until 1987 port could not be called port unless it was matured here, and this is still very much the hub of the port-wine industry.

You can of course taste port all over the city, but the

Cellar visits

For information on reservations and opening hours of the port wine lodges, visit the website of AEVP, the Association of Port Wine Companies, at www. cavesvinhodoporto.

port wine merchants only operate in Gaia and this is where tours, followed by tastings, take place. You can get here simply by crossing on the lower level of the Dom Luís I bridge – alternatively there are buses from the centre, or you can take the metro to Jardim do Morro and walk down to the waterfront.

PORT WINE LODGES

Wine lodges give you the chance to visit barrel-lined cellars, learn how port is made and, over what are normally quite generous tastings, discover how to distinguish the different aromas and flavours. Fifteen port producers are based here, and many of the famous ones have their neon names (many still British) emblazoned above the lodges. The port sold here is the same price as you'll find in shops all over the city, but the advantage is that you can try before you buy. Tastings may be accompanied (usually at extra cost) by olives and salted almonds (good with dry white port), blue cheese and chocolate (with vintage ruby port) and nutty cheese and *foie gras* (with 10-year-old tawny port). After a few tastings you'll soon realize that a bottle of port is not just for Christmas.

Some lodges require bookings, notably Graham's (see below). For others it is not always essential, but it's still a

The wine tasting halls of family-run Taylor's

good idea to call ahead to confirm times. Most tourist maps of Porto don't show the lodges, but the Gaia tourist office on the waterfront has a useful Wine Tourism Guide, with all of them marked. Most are open daily; a few close at lunch time. Tours and tastings start from about €12, but if you want to taste vintage ports expect to pay a lot more.

The port houses lining the riverfront invariably attract the most tourists. To avoid the crowds and enjoy the best views and most exclusive wine lodges, you need to climb up the hill or take a taxi. Port connoisseurs usually head up the hill to **Graham's** ③ (www.grahams-port.com), a sophisticated and newly renovated late 19th-century lodge, with a professional tour, short video, tasting rooms and an excellent restaurant (Vinum, see page 112) and shop (anyone for the 1882 vintage at €6,000 a bottle?). **Taylor's** ㉜ (www.taylor.pt), a walk or short taxi ride up Rua do Choupelo, is another top producer, dating back to 1692 and still family-run. Here you can take a fairly extensive and very informative self-guided audio tour (no booking necessary) with films, exhibits and images, ending with tastings of its Chip Dry (Extra Dry White) and LBV (Late Bottled Vintage), invented in the 1930s and 1970s respectively. If you're feeling flush, a visit could be preceded or followed by a sumptuous lunch or dinner at Taylor's Barão Fladgate restaurant, with fabulous views over Porto and the River Douro. **Churchill's** ㉝ (www.churchills-port.com), below Graham's, is smaller and more intimate than the other lodges, with cheaper tours. For a Portuguese wine lodge, try **Ferreira** ㉞ (www.sograpevinhos. com), one of the largest in Gaia and the only major port wine house to have remained in Portuguese hands since its foundation over 250 years ago (see page 69).

If time is limited and you want to taste port without a tour, head for the Sogevinus Wine Shop on the waterfront (Avenida Ramos Pinto, 280), a port-wine holding company with a good variety of ports and wines from their four brands. Prices are no higher than those you find in the port wine cellars. Another option is the very conspicuous **Espaço Porto Cruz** ㉟ (www. myportocruz.com), a swish four-storey building on the front

◎ A PORT ENTREPRENEUR

Against all the odds in a male-dominated sector, Antónia Ferreira (1811–96), affectionately known as 'A Ferreirinha' or 'Little Ferreira' (she was only 1.5 metres/4ft 11ins tall), became famous for her formidable role in port production and winemaking innovation. She was hugely energetic and ran the Ferreira company from 1844 until her death in 1896. A picture of her hangs in the Ferreira port wine lodge on Avenida de Ramos Pinto, just back from the waterfront. The diminutive port producer was almost drowned when the boat she was on capsized in the rapids of the Douro in 1861, but was saved by her crinoline which kept her afloat – unlike her unfortunate English friend, Baron de Forrester, wine merchant and owner of the boat, who drowned. A stone marks the spot on the river where he died.

with tastings on the second floor, a restaurant on the third and a panoramic 360-degree lounge on the fourth. With its comfy cushioned seats, port wines, cocktails and superlative views, this rooftop bar is a great location at sunset.

THE RIVERFRONT

There are other attractions in Gaia apart from port, notably the superb views across to Porto. These can be admired from the quayside or from the terraces of many of the cafés and restaurants. Serious foodies will be heading up the hill to Yeatman's Restaurant (see page 112), Porto's highest rated restaurant with two Michelin stars. But if all you're after is a quick bite, try the reinvented Mercado Beira Rio, just back from the riverfront, where fruit, vegetables and flowers now coexist with some seriously good food stalls.

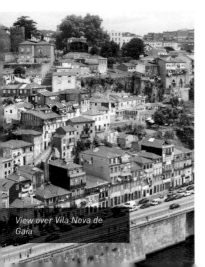

View over Vila Nova de Gaia

Moored along the river are replicas of the *barcos rabelos*, the flat-bottomed sailboats that used to bring the new port wine down from the Douro Valley in wooden casks. During the second day of the feast of São João (24th June), the *rabelos* participate in colourful races on the River Douro. Today cruise boats of all descriptions can be seen along the waterfront, including the larger craft at the western end which offer week-long cruises to the Douro Valley.

It is tempting to while away the hours on the waterfront and savour the views across the river, but spare time too for the quaint alleys behind where you'll find more local life, hole-in-the-wall tavernas and some eye-catching urban art. Rua Cândido dos Reis (going up from Sandeman's cellars) is one of the more characterful streets. To the east, the pretty Igreja de Santa Marinha, with its slender bell tower, was one of many churches in Porto remodelled by prolific Baroque architect Nicolau Nasoni.

> ### Vintage port
>
> A bottle of vintage port should be consumed within 48 hours of opening. Whether at home or in Portugal, don't pay a high price for a glass of a rare vintage port unless the bartender or waiter opens the bottle in front of you. For most establishments that's too expensive a proposition.

MOSTEIRO DA SERRA DO PILAR

The panoramic **Teleférico de Gaia** ❸ (cablecar; www.gaiacablecar.com; May–Sept 10am–8pm, 6pm off-season) climbs above the riverfront, affording peerless views of Porto and the wine lodges below. In five minutes you are at the **Jardim do Morro** ❸, an attractive and well-tended garden with lush lawns, colourful flowerbeds and stone benches where you can sit and take in the views. The gardens can also be accessed up a flight of steps from the Gaia waterfront. Presiding over Gaia on the hilltop is the **Mosteiro da Serra do Pilar** ❸ (Tue–Sun Jan–Feb, Apr–June, Sept–Dec 9.30am–5.30pm, Mar until 6.30pm, July and Aug until 7pm, with exceptions; belvedere only is free), accessed by crossing the main road (near

Mosteiro da Serra do Pilar

the metro) followed by a 5-minute climb up the hill. You can also get there from the upper level of the Dom Luís I bridge or via the metro to Jardim do Morro.

Construction of the monastery began in 1538, but due to lack of funding and political turmoil wasn't completed for over 100 years. It is a remarkable building, unique in the Iberian peninsula for its circular floor plan and cloister. Originally occupied by Augustinian Friars, its role in more recent history has been more military than religious. Strategically located over the river, it played a key role in the defence against the Napoleonic invasions. It was from the terrace here that Lord Wellesley, the future Duke of Wellington, planned his surprise attack on the French in 1809. More recently, the Liberals occupied the monastery while defending it against the Absolutists during the Portuguese Civil War (1824–34). The monastery is still a military base, so don't be surprised to see soldiers in army fatigues.

The belvedere affords spectacular views of the river and Porto, and even more spectacular ones if you climb the dome (over 100 steps) with one of the soldiers. This you can do only on a guided tour, which also covers the church, cloister and an exhibition on World Heritage Sites in the Porto region. For a reduced rate you can visit the peaceful cloister independent of a guide.

EXCURSIONS

For visitors with time to venture beyond the city, there are plenty of options. The River Douro is by far the biggest attraction, with boat trips ranging from the one-hour Six Bridges tour to a week's cruise to the port-producing upper Douro Valley. Porto is a springboard for this scenic wine-growing region, and from the city it can be reached by rail and road as well as river.

For more local trips, consider crossing the river to the simple fishing village of Alfurada or taking a vintage tram to the Atlantic-battered beaches of Foz do Douro. Short city breaks are the norm for Porto, but for those staying longer there are several other historic cities which are worth considering for a day trip: Braga, boasting Portugal's most spectacularly sited sanctuary; the historic centre of Guimarães, first capital of Portugal; attractive Amarante, on a gorge of the River Tâmega; and, to the south of Porto, the charming university city of Coimbra. All are easily reached by train.

SIX BRIDGES CRUISE

Choose a sunny day, jump on one of the boats along the quayside and enjoy a delightful hour's cruise admiring the remarkable engineering and elegance of the six city bridges. The tour also gives you glorious views of Porto. Boat tour companies have kiosks on both sides of the river, varying in price (€12–15), and some include a voucher for port-tasting at Vila Nova de Gaia.

A clear commentary in English covers the history of the bridges. First is the iconic Ponte Dom Luís I, which has connected Porto and Vila Nova de Gaia since 1886. It was designed by Théophile Seyrig, former partner of Gustave Eiffel (of Eiffel Tower fame). The photogenic two-tier structure provides a wonderful backdrop for holiday snapshots and looks spectacular illuminated at night. Originally crossed by mule-drawn carriages, it was equipped with tram tracks on the upper deck in 1905 and adapted for the metro in 2003–5. Pedestrians can cross on either deck and in summer local youngsters can be seen leaping into the river from the lower level (collecting tourist euros for encouragement). Next along is the slim, elegant **Ponte do Infante**, which with its 280 metres (919ft) arch span is the longest of the bridges over the Douro. Built in 2003, it is also the newest.

Eiffel failed in his bid for the Dom Ponte Luís I, but in the 1870s he was commissioned to design the graceful railway bridge to the east, the now inactive **Ponte Dona Maria Pia**, named after the then Queen of Portugal. It carried trains across the water until 1991. Plans to reopen it as a pedestrian and cycle bridge have never materialised. It was superseded by the futuristic **Ponte São João** (1991) which you can see just beyond it. The pillars of the newer bridge are hollow and have lifts and stairs inside to enable inspection of the structure. The old bridge has been retained as a monument and is treasured by locals.

⊙ BRIDGE CLIMBING

If you spy little figures on the Ponte da Arrábida, they will be on a guided ascent with the Porto Bridge Climb (www.portobridgeclimb.com). Anyone over 12 with a head for heights can join a (harnessed) climb up 262 steps to the top of the arch for stunning views – with a comforting shot of port wine at the top. Just beyond the bridge the river meets the ocean and you can often spot the white horses of the Atlantic in the far distance.

The boat will turn around before reaching the modern **Ponte do Freizo** (1995), but it can be seen clearly in the distance. You then head towards the Atlantic, and the last bridge is the **Ponte da Arrábida**. With a span of 270 metres (886ft), this was the largest concrete-arch bridge in the world at the time of its inauguration in 1963.

Ponte da Arrábida

FOZ DO DOURO AND MATOSINHOS

Only 5km (3 miles) northwest of Porto lies the upmarket seaside suburb of Foz do Douro (or simply 'Foz'), and just north of it, Matosinhos, a commercial centre of warehouses and docks with a huge sandy beach and an old quarter famed for fish. After a day or two of city sightseeing in Porto it's fun to hop on vintage tram No. 1, trundle along the riverside and arrive at the breezy Atlantic shore. From Foz to Matosinhos it's about an hour's walk, but you can always take the Bus No. 500 or an Uber. The metro also goes to Matosinhos.

Foz do Douro ③ means 'Mouth of the River', and this desirable suburb sits where the River Douro empties into the Atlantic. With its elegant houses, gardens with palms, beaches and long seaside promenade, Foz became a seaside resort in the 19th century and was particularly popular with the British – hence the Praia dos Ingleses. The beaches are fine for chilling out on a

Green and sculpted Jardim do Passeio Alegre

deckchair or enjoying the sunset over a cocktail, but remember that this is the Atlantic, with chilly water and big waves when it's windy – more popular with surfers than casual bathers. Beware too of the rocks that are found on most beaches.

The tram goes as far as the **Jardim do Passeio Alegre** in Foz, the delightful riverside gardens with lofty palms, ponds, fountains, sculptures and shady benches under plane trees. Behind lies the village-like Foz Velha, the old town, with attractive steep, cobbled streets. Hidden away here and rather unexpected is one of the best restaurants in the region, the Pedro Lemos (see page 113). On the seafront the prominent **Fort of São João da Foz** (Mon–Fri 9am–5.30pm; free) was built in 1570–1647 to protect the coast and the mouth of the River Douro. There is not much to see inside, but the ramparts and watchtower afford fine views of the coast. These are particularly dramatic on windy days when the Atlantic rollers crash against the lighthouse. A stroll on the promenade takes you alongside sandy and rocky beaches, with bar terraces for enjoying the ocean views. These are very popular spots at sunset. Above the Praia do Molhe is the elegant 1930s **Pérgola da Foz**, modelled on the pergola of the Promenade des Anglais in Nice.

If you carry on north you come to the Praça de Gonçalves Zarco, a large roundabout overlooked by the 17th-century Forte de São Francisco Zavier, better known as **Castelo do Queijo** (Cheese Castle; Tue–Fri 1–5pm, Sat and Sun 11am–5pm), so-called because of the shape of the rock it sits on. Opposite is **Sea Life Porto**, a large aquarium which is always a hit with youngsters (see page 93), while spreading inland is the vast **Parque da Cidade** (City Park), the main green lung of Porto. Extending over 33 hectares (83 acres), this is an oasis for city dwellers, with a wealth of flora and fauna, small lakes with ducks and geese, bike paths and sports fields.

The huge beach at **Matosinhos** ⓐ is sheltered by the harbour and is a popular spot for learner surfers. There are about six surfing schools here, as well other watersports on offer. Being so close to Porto and with easy access by metro, the sands get packed in high season.

From the waterfront you can see the gleaming

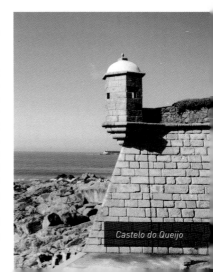

Castelo do Queijo

Terminal de Cruzeiros (Cruiseship Terminal), a brand new, swirling white structure which has won awards for architecture and design. It was designed by Luís Pedro Silva and has witnessed a significant increase in cruise ships to Porto. The interior is super slick, but unless you are a passenger you can only visit on the weekly guided tour (Sun 9.30am–1pm). The evocative sculpture behind the beach, *the Tragédia do Mar*, honours the victims of the shipwreck of four trawlers in 1947, when 150 fishermen lost their lives.

⊙ LEÇA DA PALMEIRA

Across the harbour from Matosinhos at Leça da Palmeira are two architectural attractions, one of which will also appeal to gourmets. Merging seamlessly with the rocks and secluded on a wooded hill overlooking the sea is the Piscina das Marés (Sea Pool; mid-June–mid-Sept; daily 9am–7pm), designed in 1966 by leading Portuguese architect, Álvaro Siza Vieira, a Pritzker prize winner who was born in Matosinhos and is best known for the Contemporary Art Museum at Serralves, Porto. The Piscina das Marés has a remarkably contemporary feel even though it was designed over 50 years ago. There are two beautiful seawater pools, one for adults, one for children. Another structure by the same architect, 1.5km (1 mile) to the north, is the Casa de Chá de Boa Nova (Avenida da Liberdade No. 1681). This is not your normal tea house *(casa de chà)*; in fact, it's a sleek structure built into the rocks above the sea with gourmet dishes by one of Portugal's best known chefs, Rui Paula. The building was classified as a national monument in 2011.

Enjoying the sunshine at Leça da Palmeira

The excellent modern tourist office by the beach has a useful booklet in English on Matosinhos. The port brands itself WBF, 'World's Best Fish', and helpful staff here will point you in the direction of the nearby fish restaurants and market. You'll soon see the fish being grilled on barbecues along the Rua dos Heróis de França. Don't go expecting elegant interiors and picturesque sea views. This is an authentic workaday place, formerly full of canned fish factories (some still survive), and most of the restaurants are family-run no-frills affairs with chalked-up menus in Portuguese. You can still eat reasonably cheaply, although with menus appearing in English and a new regulation stipulating glassed-in terraces along the street (health and safety), prices are rising. A whole range of fish and seafood is on offer and helpings are huge. Often half portions suffice.

Locals buy the fish from the dock opposite the fish restaurants. You won't see many tourists, but if you're self-catering or want to watch the action there is nothing stopping you joining the locals. You can also see the fish laid out on the lower level of the modern **Mercado de Matosinhos** nearby, although early morning is the best time to go. On the level above are stalls of fresh fruit and veg, along with cages of chickens, cockerels, ducks and rabbits.

AFURADA

Beyond the Arrábida bridge, close to where the River Douro meets the Atlantic, you can cross the river to explore the fishing village of **Afurada** ⑪ in Vila Nova de Gaia. Get there on the small Flor de Gás ferry (from Cais do Ouro; 7am–7.30pm every 15–30 mins depending on season; €2 each way). If you arrive at lunchtime, wafts of charcoal-grilled sardines and squid will

The modern arched ceiling of Mercado de Matosinhos

greet you as you step off the ferry. Along the front are fishing boats, trawlers and nets, with noisy gulls hovering overhead for fishy titbits. It's hard to go wrong when it comes to restaurants here. All will serve you fresh fish, whether it's the basic Café Vapor on the waterfront, the popular Taberna São Pedro or the new Armezem de Peize opposite the market, where you choose from an enticing display of fish and seafood or opt for a fish cataplana.

If you're wondering about all the lines of washing flapping in the breeze on the seafront, the concrete building nearby is a communal washhouse where locals still come to do the laundry. They each have their own washing line and nothing ever gets nicked. There's a low-key Interpretive Centre with fishing boats and marine memorabilia donated by the villagers, and a swish new marina that feels slightly out of place. You can take a bike across on the ferry and from Afurada cycle all the way to the beaches of Espinho (most of it by the sea), passing the Douro Estuary Natural Reserve en route (see page 96).

DOURO VALLEY

About 80km (60 miles) upstream from Porto the River Douro, or 'Golden River', twists through deep-cleft gorges, terraced with vineyards. Birthplace of port wine, the scenic **Vale do Douro** ⑫ was classified by Unesco as a World Heritage Site in 2001. The schist soil and the climate are ideal for the growing of grapes, which produce Douro wines and the famous ports. The wine is made here, then after six months it is transported to the cooler climes of Porto to be aged in its cellars. It is only in recent years that the region has opened up to eno-tourism. Some of the quintas (wine estates) offer guided tours and tastings, and a few are open for overnight stays. The best times to visit the region, for the colours and climate, are spring and

The Douro Valley

autumn. The Douro Valley has a climate of hot dry summers and severe winters. Locals in this region sum up their climate as 'nine months of winter, three months of hell'!

As a visitor to the Douro Valley, you are faced with a bewildering choice of options. You can go independently by road, rail or river; do a combination of river and rail; or, if time is tight, take a single-day guided excursion by minibus, which will include the best of the scenery, a visit to a couple of vineyards and an hour's boat trip on the most scenic part of the river. With time in hand, go for a couple of days, stay at a *quinta* (wine estate) and enjoy the scenery, the culture and the cuisine at leisure.

A day's boat trip might seem the most appealing option, but beware that the craft are very crowded in season and availability of seats on the upper deck (with the best views) are limited. Avoid boats that only go as far as Régua – this way you'll only see a bit of the best scenery. There's also a magnificent railway line, the Linha do Douro, which departs from São Bento station and goes as far as the tiny village of Pocinho in the Alto Douro (3.5 hours). For the first hour it's fairly non-descript suburbia and countryside, but after Régua the railway follows a spectacular course beside the river with glorious views of the terraced vineyards on the steep hillsides.

There is not much to see in Pocinho itself and a more popular option is a train to Pinhão followed by a boat trip along a scenic stretch of the Douro. Bustling Régua, where cruises stop off, also offers river excursions and is home to the Douro Museum, dedicated to wine. Whichever way you go, a day trip by rail requires an early start, and you will need to be highly organised with timing.

Hiring a car has the obvious advantage of flexibility, and this way you are able to enjoy the best of the scenery. However, driving is not for the faint-hearted. Roads are steep, winding and slow-going, so drivers won't be able to enjoy the views (the N-222 between Pinhão and Régua was voted the World's Best Drive by Avis in 2015), nor taste or imbibe with abandon.

Boat trips along the Douro open up the wine-growing region

Drinking in the view

 # WHAT TO DO

ENTERTAINMENT

Porto has seen a huge surge in entertainment and especially nightlife options in recent years. The city stages some great music, both classical and contemporary, and downtown Porto is a hive of lively cafés, bars and late-night clubs. In summer look out for flyers advertising concerts in various venues around the city, some of which are free.

CONCERTS, THEATRE, OPERA AND CINEMA

The iconic **Casa da Música** (Av. da Boavista 604-610, www. casadamusica.com) is the city's premier venue for local and international classical and contemporary music, and is home to the leading Orquestra Nacional do Porto. The avant-garde concert hall, which opened in 2005, has been a huge success and has helped regenerate the Boavista area. Prices for concerts are very reasonable and some are free. In summer, the **Jardim do Palácio de Cristal** and **Serralves Park** stage open-air concerts. The 3,000-seat **Coliseu do Porto** (Rua de Passos Manuel 137; www.coliseu.pt) stages international events, from rock and indie concerts to musicals and dance productions. **Hard Club** in Praça Infante Dom Henrique (www. hardclubporto.com), within the restored 19th-century Ferreira Borges Market, is a dynamic centre with a wide-ranging programme of concerts, dance and theatre events, films, art exhibitions and educational activities. Quite a few events are free of charge.

Local theatrical performances are nearly always in Portuguese. The **Teatro Nacional São João** (see page 42) is the city's main theatre, with concerts, ballet and occasionally opera, as well as plays.

Multiplexes around the city show mainstream films in English or with English subtitles.

NIGHTLIFE

Night spots have been springing up all over the city in recent years, with one seemingly on every street corner. Formerly derelict town houses or warehouses are now brimming with life, converted, often in vintage style, into cafés, bars or night-clubs – or a combination of all three. Few of the clubs show any signs of life before 10 or 11pm, closing around 4 or even 6am. Admission fees range from €5–20 and usually include a drink, though special events will cost extra. Remember to take cash as many places don't accept card.

An irresistible spot for a sun-downer is the Ribeira water-front, watching the twinkling lights across the river from one of the many cafés. In downtown Porto locals tend to drift from bar to bar, with drink in hand (many venues have plastic cups). Students tend to start their bar crawls at the famous **Café Piolho** (see page 111) by the university. For a late night out the place to go is 'the Galerias', namely the Rua Galeria de Paris and Rua Cândido dos Reis quarter, which is packed with nightclubs, jazz venues and watering holes of every descrip-tion. For cocktails created by top mixologists and a cool vibe, try the **Royal Cocktail Club** at Rua da Fábrica 105.

Across the river at Vila Nova de Gaia, **Dick's Bar** at the famous Yeatman Hotel has one of the best cellars in Portugal. The fine wood-aged and vintage ports are available by the bot-tle or glass. With the plush sofas, jaw-dropping views of Porto (and live music Thu–Sat), you're likely to linger all evening. Another Gaia option is the panoramic riverside Terrace Lounge

360º at the top of the contemporary **Espaço Porto Cruz** (www.myportocruz.com) at Largo Miguel Bombarda 23. The superb views of the Porto across the Douro can be enjoyed over a cocktail or glass of port. Sunset is the ideal time to come.

Cálem wine lodge

Fado

Portugal's musical expression of longing and sorrow is from Lisbon and Coimbra rather than Porto. But there is plenty of *fado vadio*, or amateur fado, sung at *fado* houses, tavern-like restaurants offering an evening of *fado*, Portuguese food and wine. The plaintive Portuguese song, literally 'fate' translated into music, is based on a story or poem and is accompanied by the Portuguese 12-stringed guitar or *viola* (acoustic Spanish guitar). Lamentation of lost loves, crossed lovers or the forces of destiny are all characteristic themes. Sung by professionals, these chants are plangent, haunting and intensely moving, though to the unattuned ear they can sound strange and monotonous (hence the occasional jollification of traditional *fado* for the benefit of tourists). The **Cálem Port Wine Lodge** on the waterfront at Vila Nova de Gaia is one of the main *fado* venues in Porto, staging concerts from Tuesday to Sunday evenings with a cellar tour and tasting included in the price (€21). Visit www.fadoinporto.com for bookings. Alternatively, watch a *fado* show over dinner at the **Taberna Real do Fado** (Rua Dr Barbosa de Castro 58; www.realfado.pt) or **Casa da Mariquinhas** (Rua de São Sebastião 25; www.casadamariquinhas.pt). There is usually a minimum charge.

SHOPPING

Porto is becoming increasingly cosmopolitan, with modern shopping centres and high-street chains, but alongside international names are young Portuguese designers showing off their latest creations as well as eye-catching vintage-style shops. In the streets of Baixa you can still find the occasional old-fashioned haberdashery, little altered in 100 years, and thriving old-school grocery shops stacked with cheeses, spicy sausages and bottles of wine and port.

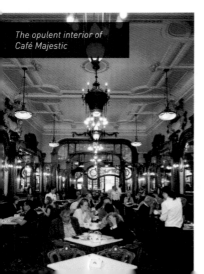

The opulent interior of Café Majestic

The favourite street for fashion is the **Rua de Santa Catarina**, lined with national and international chains, designer boutiques, jewellery stores, shoe shops and vintage shops. When it's time to take a break, head either for the famous **Café Majestic** (see page 111) at No. 112, where the tourist queue normally spills out on to the road, or Nata Lisboa at No. 499, known for its creamy, crispy pasteis de nata (custard tarts).

The rejuvenated and pedestrianised **Rua das Flores** is now an appealing shopping street, with fashionable cafés, chocolate shops, boutiques, jewellers and antiquarian booksellers. Few can resist the exquisite delights of the **Chocolataria Ecuador** or the hand-crafted soaps, candles and cologne from **Claus Porto**. Out of the centre, Boavista is known for international designer stores and luxury items, but lacks the atmosphere of the more central, older streets, with their Portuguese shops.

> ### Pastéis de nata
>
> You can't go to Portugal and not sample the custard tarts (pastéis de nata, in Porto often simply called nata). The best ones have a crispy case, a creamy sweet filling and have just come out of the oven. The secret is butter (never margarine), eggs, plenty of sugar, no preservatives – and preferably weeks of training to knead and fold the pastry.

HANDICRAFTS AND SOUVENIRS

Azulejos, the hand-painted ceramic tiles that have been decorating Portugal's walls through the centuries, make popular souvenirs. Some places will paint tiles to order if you have a particular design in mind, or copy a photograph. Antique azulejos are highly sought after and very expensive, but you can buy reproductions of well-known historic designs. Portuguese pottery and ceramics are found in many designs and colours, from fine porcelain to folksy earthenware and the vividly coloured Barcelos rooster.

For genuine Portuguese products head for **A Vida Portuguesa** (Rua Galeria de Paris 20; www.avidaportuguesa.

com), a vast emporium packed with traditional Portuguese products, from retro-wrapped soaps and traditional ceramics to attractively canned sardines. **Armazém**, at Rua de Miragaia 93, in a converted port warehouse by the river, is a very cool concept store combining fashion with artwork, antiques and Portuguese-designed accessories and ceramics.

CORK AND LEATHER

Portugal produces over half the world's cork in terms of the raw material, more in terms of the finished product. While more and more wine bottlers are using screw caps, new uses have been found for eco-friendly Portuguese cork. You can find finely crafted bags, baseball caps, lampshades, hats, handbags and even umbrellas. The Portuguese leather industry

Goods for sale at Armazém

is known throughout the world and belts, bags, purses, wallets, luggage and shoes are good buys. Try the **Feeting Room**, a cool concept store at Largo dos Lóios 86, where Portuguese shoes and boots are beautifully displayed, along with clothing and accessories.

ART GALLERIES

Northwest of the centre, the Rua de Miguel Bombarda and the surrounding area is the place to come for hip galleries, concept stores, vintage clothing, organic food shops and trendy accessories. **Ó! Galeria** at No. 61 is one of the largest galleries, with regularly changing exhibitions of drawings, illustrations, books and magazines, mostly by young and up-and-coming illustrators. At No. 285, the **CCB** (Centro Comercial Bombarda; Mon–Sat noon–8pm) is a small sleek mall and creative hub of independent Portuguese boutiques and galleries. Note that most shops in the quarter don't open until noon.

BOOKS

The **Livraria Lello** (Rua das Carmelitas 144; www.livrarialello. pt; vouchers available online or from the corner shop up the road, redeemable against purchases) near the Clérigos Tower is a must-see for any visitor to Porto (see page 46). The Art Nouveau bookstore dates back to 1906 and is rated one of the most beautiful in the world, so be prepared for crowds. The fabulous collection includes limited-edition books.

GASTRONOMY

The atmospheric **Mercado do Bolhão**, dating from 1914, has always been the place to go for the freshest of fish, meat, fruit and veg, as well as chickens, tripe and rabbits. But the wrought-iron market hall, in dire need of restoration, closed in 2018 for at least two years. With modern shops and restaurants planned for the upper tier, it is unlikely to reopen as the earthy market of yore. But the streets around have some enticing, old-fashioned grocery stores, such as the 100-year-old **A Pérola do Bolhão**, with its fetching Art Nouveau facade on Rua Formosa, opposite the market. This and other delis will vacuum-pack fresh produce to make it easier for you to take home. **Comer e Chorar Por Mais** ('Eat and Cry for More') at Rua Formosa 300 is another gourmet grocery, jam-packed

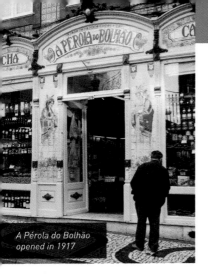
A Pérola do Bolhão opened in 1917

with hams, cheeses, olive oil, honey, fine wines and freshly made bread from the wood oven.

The Portuguese have a very sweet tooth, and the Portuenses are no exception. The city has myriad patisseries which lure you in with their displays of cakes and pastries. Beware though – they can be very sickly. One of the best confectioners is **Arcádia** on Rua do Almada 63 (west of Aliados), family-run since 1933 and famous for chocolate linguas de gato (cat's tongues) and chocolate/port bonbons, made in partnership with port-producers, Calém.

Port is the obvious souvenir to take back home if luggage permits. If not, it can be shipped for you – at a price. Vintage port from the most select years is what connoisseurs and collectors seek, but there are much cheaper bottles available. Look for aged tawny, LBV (late bottle vintages) or a bottle of white port. The dry version of the latter is now popularly drunk in Porto with tonic water and a slice of orange or lemon, especially in the summer months. Dozens of outlets sell port and you can try it at port wine lodges, tasting rooms and some of the shops. **Portologia**, at Rua de São João 28–30, just up from the Ribeira waterfront, is a small and cosy port-tasting place with knowledgeable staff to guide you through the vast range. They have over 200 ports, mainly from the smaller producers, and offer a set price for tastings so you can taste before purchasing (eg 6 tastings for €25 or €35, depending on the quality of the port).

For tasting and/or buying regional wines as well as port, head for the **Instituto dos Vinhos do Douro e do Porto** (Douro Wine and Port Institute; Rua Ferreira Borges 27; www.ivdp. pt). With a wine shop, small museum and tastings, this is an excellent introduction to port and Douro wines.

CHILDREN'S PORTO

With its vintage trams, funiculars and river trips, Porto offers some great ways to entertain children around the city. Take them on Tram No. 1, which rattles alongside the river to the beaches at Foz do Douro, or on a boat trip to see the six bridges of Porto (see page 27). The top children's attractions in the city are the **World of Discoveries** (see page 54) and **Sea Life** (1a Rua Particular do Castelo do Queijo; www.sealife-porto. pt; Mon–Fri 10am–6pm, Sat–Sun 10am–6.15pm, last entry 45 mins before closing), a large aquarium where you can hold sea urchins and come nose to nose with sharks, rays and turtles.

Porto has plenty of green spaces where children can let off steam. The **Jardim do Palácio de Cristal** has a lake, artificial caves and peacocks strutting around. Further west, the vast **Parque da Cidade** (City Park), the green lung of the city, stretches as far as the coast and is a favourite spot for locals to stroll, jog, cycle or picnic. The park has ponds with ducks, swans and geese, as well as a Water Pavilion which featured in Lisbon's Expo '98. Children can have fun with the interactive games, aimed to educate in the importance of water. Exhibits show how a tornado is formed and teach little minds about the water cycle.

Competing for the ball at the Estádio do Dragão

In Vila Nova de Gaia, the **Santo Inácio Zoo** (www.zoosantoinacio.com) has a free shuttle bus service operating four times a day between April and October, departing near Porto's Sé and taking around 15 minutes. The zoo is home to around 300 species and includes a lion enclosure with a glass tunnel where lions walk above you. The animals are not too restricted and there are lakes, pleasant green areas and prairie dogs roaming free.

SPORTS/OUTDOOR PURSUITS

FOOTBALL

FC Porto (or simply Porto) is one of 'the Big Three' in Portugal, alongside Lisbon's Benfica and Sporting CP. In international matches, Porto is the most decorated team in

Portugal. They won the UEFA European Champions League (or European Cup) in 1987 and 2004, the UEFA Super Cup in 1987, the UEFA Cup/European League in 2003 and 2011 and the Intercontinental Cup in 1987 and 2004. Local supporters are called Portistas.

Home matches are played at the **Estádio do Dragão** (metro Estádio do Dragão; www.fcporto.pt), which was built 4km (2.5 miles) northeast of the city centre for the 2004 European Championships. Stadium tours with audio guides in seven languages are available on non-match days (on the hour Tue–Sun 11am–5pm, Monday 3–5pm) and include entrance to a museum on the club's history.

☉ THE LONGEST NIGHT OF THE YEAR

If – out of the blue – someone hits you on the head with a leek or a squeaky plastic hammer, you'll know it's the Festa de São João. This festival, with strong pagan traditions (despite celebrating St John the Baptist, patron saint of the city), takes place annually on the night of 23rd/24th June. Thousands of partygoers descend on the centre of Porto to make merry. Streets are strung with bunting, colourful lights sparkle in the squares, wine flows and sardines are barbecued on every street corner. Street parties, free concerts and dancing are all part of the scene. At midnight, a dazzling firework display erupts over the River Douro. The revellers who are still going drift along the riverside to Foz to watch the sunrise in the early morning. Fortunately for all, 24th June is a public holiday in Porto and the climax of the festa is the colourful regatta of the barcos rabelos on the River Douro.

SWIMMING AND SURFING

The chilly waters of the Atlantic and the choppy seas tend to put off casual swimmers, but there are opportunities for surfers and plentiful places to just chill out. The best beach near Porto is Espinho, 20km (12.5 miles) to the south of the city and accessed in about half an hour by rail from Porto. It's an 8km (5-mile) stretch, particularly popular with surfers. Closer to Porto, Foz do Douro has easily accessible beaches with sand, but most also have rocky outcrops. Sun loungers are normally available to hire and there are plenty of beaches with bars and snacks. Matosinhos has a large sandy beach which attracts learner surfers but, being close to a big port, it's not everyone's first choice. Further north are better sandy beaches at Vila do Conde and Póvoa de Varzim. The popular surfing beaches have surf schools which hire out gear and provide group or private lessons. The most appealing swimming pools in the area are the sea pools at Leça da Palmeira (see page 78), carved into the rocks.

BIRDWATCHING

The **Reserva Natural Local do Estuário do Douro** (dawn–dusk, www.parquebiologico.pt; free) is a small nature reserve on the Douro estuary in Vila Nova de Gaia. It is home to over 200 species of birds, among them kingfishers, herons, white egrets, sandpipers, plovers, red knots and blue throats.

GOLF

The oldest golf club in the Iberian peninsula, founded by the British in the late 19th century, is the Oporto Golf Club in Espinho, Vila Nova de Gaia, 18km (11 miles) from the centre of Porto. Also in Vila Nova de Gaia is the 9-hole Miramar Golf Club (Av. Sacadura Cabral, Arcozelo), 12km (7.5 miles) from Porto's centre.

CALENDAR OF EVENTS

Fantasporto (or 'Fantas') February/March. A 10-day international film festival screening fantasy, sci-fi and horror movies.

Queima das Fitas do Porto (Porto's Burning of the Ribbons) May. Final-year student festival featuring concerts, academic parades and other events which now involve the entire city.

Festa de São João June 23rd/24th. Porto's biggest event of the year (see page 95) and part of the Festas da Cidade, which has events and entertainment throughout the month.

Regata dos Rabelos June 24th (coinciding with the Festa de São João). A regatta of the barcos rabelos (wooden sail boats) which once ferried port wine down the River Douro.

Serralves em Festa Early June. Forty hours of non-stop dance, music, theatre and exhibitions in Serralves Park; also in Baixa. This is the largest contemporary arts festival in Portugal with both international and Portuguese performers (www.serralvesemfesta.com).

Nos Primavera Sound June. Two-day open-air music festival in Parque da Cidade (www.nosprimaverasound.com).

Feira do Livro do Porto (Porto Book Fair) June. A long-established event, traditionally held at the Jardim do Palácio de Cristal.

São Pedro da Afurada 29 June. Festival held in honour of St Peter, patron saint of fishermen, at the fishing village of Afurada, Vila Nova de Gaia.

Festival Internacional de Folclore Cidade Late July/early August. Week-long folklore festival.

LGBT Porto Pride First or second week of July. LGBT celebration first held in Porto in 2001, with a parade since 2006.

Porto Wine Fest July. Wine tastings and gastronomic events on the riverbank of Vila Nova de Gaia.

Noites Ritual Rock Last weekend of August. Rock concerts by local bands held in the Jardim do Palácio de Cristal.

Porta Jazz Early December. Free jazz concerts (www.portajazz.com).

Christmas December. Fairs and markets around the city.

EATING OUT

Culinary hotspots have been popping up all over the city in recent years, and there is now a great diversity in the dining scene. You can choose from trusty hole-in-the-wall *tascas* (taverns), tapas bars and new on-trend restaurants where creative chefs have developed a more refined, cosmopolitan style of cuisine. The region is rich in culinary delights, with fish from the Atlantic, pork and dairy produce from the remote Trás-os-Montes ('Beyond the Mountains') and the famous port and wines from the valley of the Upper Douro. But Porto's own specialities are still very much on the menu. You won't have to go far to find '*tripas à moda do Porto*' (Port-style tripe) or the '*francesinha*', a multi-layered gut-busting sandwich (see page 105).

WHERE TO EAT

Formal restaurants are few and far between, the emphasis being more on smaller places serving *petiscos* (smaller versions of large dishes, like tapas but usually larger). Two or three of these can provide a decent meal, there are plenty to choose from and it's the perfect way of trying several regional dishes. Typical *petiscos* are *pataniscas* (delicious little salt-cod croquettes), *gambas al ajillo* (garlic shrimps) or *salada de polvo* (octopus salad).

Tascas are typically found in the narrow streets of the old town, and are traditionally family-run joints with paper tablecloths, serving hearty helpings of authentic Portuguese cuisine. Often one portion suffices for two. Some *tascas* have seen a modern makeover in recent years, but they are still faithful to local fare, albeit with a modern twist. The inconspicuous back-street eateries are usually better value than the touristy restaurants and the cafés strung along the quaysides, on both sides of the river.

A *restaurante* covers a whole range of eateries, from sumptuous to basic. A *churrasqueira* is a grill, typically serving simple fare such as grilled sardines or half chickens. A *marisqueira* will specialise in seafood; a *cervejaria* is a beer house, which normally serves seafood and steaks as well as a good choice of beers; and a *confeitaria* is a patisserie. Prices across the range of restaurants are fairly affordable by the standards of European capitals.

Porto has a vibrant café culture, with countless places offering the simple pleasure of a cup of good coffee and creamy *pastéis de nata* (custard tarts) or other freshly made pastries.

The 'francesinha', a Porto speciality

Pre-starters and starters

No sooner are you seated than unrequested pre-starters such as bread, fresh cheese, cured ham, olives and maybe fish paté or octopus salad will arrive on the table. They may seem free, but they are not. It may only be a euro or two for bread (often delicious Broa or corn bread) or olives, but it could be €5 for the cheese or meat. These often make appetising starters, but you have the option (if you're strong-willed!) to leave them untouched and not be charged.

Local starters include seafood dishes, hearty soups, cured and smoked hams, sausages and salamis, often heavily smoked and spiced. The ubiquitous *caldo verde* soup, made with finely shredded cabbage, potatoes, onion, garlic and sometimes sausage too, features on menus from the classiest restaurants down to the humblest *tasca*. Thick bread soups are a meal in themselves and include the classic *açorda de marisco*, a spicy, garlicky shellfish stew.

Fish and seafood

Bacalhau à Gomes de Sá

Seafood enthusiasts are spoilt for choice. You'll find sardines and squid, clams and crabs, sea bass, lobster and sole. The humble but noble Portuguese sardine is an inexpensive standard, and served with a hunk of local rustic bread and a bottle of house wine, you can still feast well on a small budget. The sardine season, when the fish are at their fattest, is from May to October. Seafood restaurants generally sell shellfish by weight, giving the price in euros per kilo. Among the specialities are *caldeirada de peixe*, a rich seafood stew, and *arroz de marisco*, a delicious seafood rice dish with crab, lobster claws, prawns, clams and cockles. Clams are often served simply with crushed garlic cloves, fresh coriander and white wine: *amêijoas à Bulhão Pato*. Squid (*lulas*) come stuffed with rice, olives, tomato and onion, though the large squid are often grilled and served on a skewer with prawns (*gambas*). You can't normally tell from the menu whether the fish is fresh or frozen, but you can always ask the waiter for the catch of the day. Don't assume the bass and bream are from the high seas – much of it is farmed these days. Serious fish aficionados should head for Matosinhos, famous for its fresh fish restaurants (see page 75).

> ### Portuguese portions
>
> The locals have large appetites. Beware of diet-busting patisserie and huge helpings, especially of casserole dishes of say cod, *cataplanas* or tripe, where one portion could easily feed two or even three. Some restaurants will offer a half portion, *uma meia dose*, and unless you have a very large appetite the smaller portion is usually sufficient.

The national favourite fish is strangely neither Portuguese nor eaten fresh: it's dried, salted cod or *bacalhau* and is served in 100, 365 or 1,000 different ways, depending on the teller's taste for hyperbole. Records show that the Portuguese were fishing Newfoundland's Grand Banks for cod within just a few years of Columbus's discovery of America. They were soon to discover that by salting cod at sea they could make it last the long voyage home.

It was then sun-dried into board-stiff slabs that could be kept for months. The Portuguese now import *bacalhau* from Norway, just to be able to meet their annual demands. This, of course, puts the price of salt cod – once an inexpensive staple of the national diet – beyond the reach of the very people it sustained for centuries. All these once-humble recipes are served today in the most expensive restaurants. The Porto speciality is *Bacalhau à Gomes de Sá*: flaky chunks of cod baked with parsley, potatoes, onions and olives and garnished with grated hard-boiled egg.

Meat dishes

Although the emphasis is on fish and seafood, restaurants do not skimp on meat. The ubiquitous *Tripas à Moda do Porto* is a thick, hearty stew with offal, white beans and sausages, though every Porto family has its own recipe. The people of Porto are known as *Tripeiros* or tripe-eaters (see page 18), but some of the new chefs are catering more for tourists and dropping tripe from the menu. Pork is sweet and tender; ham (*presunto* and *fiambre*) and sausages (*salsichas*) are highly prized in Portugal; and charcuterie features prominently in soups and stews. *Alheira* is a sausage made of meats other than pork (usually chicken) with bread and

Homemade sausages for sale

spices. It was created by the Jewish community in northeast Portugal during the Inquisition to give the impression they had converted to Christianity by eating pork – the traditional ingredient for a Portuguese sausage. *Arouquesa* veal is wonderfully succulent and chicken (*frango*) is popular and versatile, whether stewed in wine sauce, fried, roasted or barbecued. *Feijoada* is not nearly as elaborate or ritualised as it is in Portugal's former colony of Brazil, where it is a national dish, but it's still a tasty stew of pigs' trotters and sausage, white beans and cabbage.

> **Fixed menus**
>
> To fill up for a few euros, opt for the *menu do dia* (fixed menu) offered by many restaurants at lunch time, often at a fraction of the cost of the evening meal. A set menu typically offers soup and bread, a main course and a glass of wine. Also well worth trying is the *prato do dia* or dish of the day.

Desserts and cheese

The Portuguese have a passion for all things sweet, and Porto is packed with *pastelerias* (patisseries), bakeries and cafés selling wickedly calorific cakes and pastries. Many of these are loaded with sugar and egg yolks. It was nuns of Portugal in the 17th and 18th centuries who became famous for creating egg desserts, which explains names such as 'bacon from heaven' (*toucinho do céu*), nuns' tummies (*barriga da freira*) and angels' cheeks (*papos d'anjo*). As in the rest of Portugal, the crispy and creamy custard tarts, called *pastéis de nata* (in Porto simply nata) are firm favourites and feature in every patisserie and on nearly every menu. Egg desserts and pastries are flavoured with cinnamon, lemon, orange or almonds, and each is shaped

Porto is famous for its wine and port

in its own traditional way, for example like miniature haystacks, or occasionally even lamprey eels. The Portuguese so love this ugly river fish that they make golden egg effigies of it for festive occasions.

The Portuguese find that nothing complements – or follows – an egg sweet as well as a silky, syrupy wine, usually a vintage port or a Madeira, but better still a good, strong cup of coffee to cut the sweetness.

The most savoury Portuguese cheeses are from ewes' milk. Serra da Estrela is the richest and most expensive cheese and can be served fresh or cured.

Wine

Portuguese wine has come on in leaps and bounds in recent years. The Douro Valley, traditionally best known for port, now produces some wonderfully robust and full-bodied reds, as well as some excellent whites. From the Minho region comes *Vinho Verde*, a refreshing, slightly sparkling young wine which goes down a treat with seafood on a sunny day. *Vinho espumante* is Portuguese sparkling wine, packaged in a Champagne-shaped bottle. Most are sweetish, but you can find some quite dry versions too. When ordering wine you can't go far wrong with the house wine (*vinho da casa*). Ask the waiter for *tinto* (red), *branco* (white) or *rosado* (pink).

Port

Fortified port wine has tantalised palates around the world since the British began exporting it in the 17th century. It comes in many forms, from ruby, tawny, white, rosé and Late Bottled Vintage (LBV) through to Vintage Port, generally considered to be *la crème de la crème*. Before dinner, try a P&T, *porto tónico* (white port and tonic), which is currently all the rage as a summer cocktail. The wine tasting lodges are all in Vila Nova de Gaia, across the Douro from Porto, offering wine tours and tastings (see page 66), but there are countless places in Porto to taste port, often with a sommelier on hand to explain the nuances of smooth tawny ports, fruity rubies and sweet or dry whites. The Port and Douro Wines Institute (see page 33) is a good place to sample them.

⊙ PORTO'S SANDWICH SPECIAL

The *francesinha* or 'little Frenchie' is a glorified sandwich consisting of chunks of steak, cured ham and sausage between slices of white bread, swathed in melted cheese, drenched in a thick spicy tomato and beer sauce, topped with a fried egg and (optionally) accompanied by French fries! It sounds more American than Portuguese, but in fact was invented in the 1950s by an emigrant returning from France where he had worked as a chef. Back in Portugal, he decided to try an elaborate version of the *croque monsieur* for the Portuguese. Locals all have their favourite *francesinha* restaurant, usually based on the quality of the meat and the sauce (a secret recipe that varies from place to place). You can find the dish in dozens of cafés and restaurants – just make sure you don't have to eat another meal on the same day!

Other drinks

Super Bock beer, brewed in Porto, is good and refreshing, very like Lisbon's Sagres. If you want a draft beer and want to sound like a local, ask for a *fino*. As in many other parts of Europe, Portugal has followed the fashion for craft beers and there are plenty of different types to try.

Coffee

Coffee houses are a Portuguese national institution, a gathering place morning, noon and night. This is not surprising in a country whose former colonies – Brazil and Angola – still produce some of the finest coffee beans in the world. The choice may be a *cimbalino*, a powerful espresso, or a *carioca*, a weaker version, which with a drop of milk is a *garoto*. If you want plenty of milk, ask for a *galão*, which comes small (*pequeno*) or tall (*grande*).

TO HELP YOU ORDER...

Could we have a table? **Queremos uma mesa?**
Do you have a set-price menu? **Tem uma ementa turística?**
I'd like a/an/some... **Queria**...

beer **uma cerveja**
the bill **a conta**
bread **pão**
butter **manteiga**
dessert **sobremesa**
fish **peixe**
fruit **fruta**
ice-cream **gelado**
meat **carne**
the menu **a carta**
milk **leite**
mineral water **água mineral**

napkin **guardanapo**
pepper **pimenta**
potatoes **batatas**
salad **salada**
salt **sal**
sandwich **sanduíche**
sauce **molho**
soup **sopa**
sugar **açúcar**
tea **chá**
vegetables **legumes**
wine **vinho**
wine list **carta de vinos**

MENU READER

alho garlic
amêijoas baby clams
arroz rice
assado roast, baked
bacalhau cod
besugo sea bream
dobrada tripe
dourada sea bass
feijões beans
frito fried
gambas prawns
lagosta spiny lobster
lenguado sole

lombo fillet
lulas squid
mariscos shellfish
mexilhões mussels
ostras oysters
ovo egg
pescada hake
pescadinha whiting
polvos baby octopus
queijo cheese
salmonete red mullet
truta trout
vitela veal

PLACES TO EAT

The prices indicated here are for a two-course meal with wine for one person. (Note that some fish or shellfish dishes will be more expensive). Tax (IVA) is included. Restaurants listed here accept major credit cards unless cash only is stated.

€€€€	over 45 euros
€€€	30–45 euros
€€	20–30 euros
€	below 20 euros

RIBEIRA

Adega de São Nicolau €€ *Rua de São Nicolau; tel: 222 008 232; Mon–Sat noon–11pm* On a narrow alley just back from the riverfront and a favourite with the locals, this cosy restaurant is designed as an up-turned hull of a ship. Authentic Porto dishes are plentiful, including salted codfish croquettes, the tripe Porto-style (one helping is easily big enough for two), octopus rice and melt-in-the-mouth *Aronquera* veal steak.

Bacalhau €€ *Muro dos Bacalhoeiros 153-155; tel: 222 010 521; www.bacalhauporto.pt; Sun–Thu 11am–11pm, Fri and Sat 11am–midnight* No surprises as to the speciality here. You can start with *sopa alentejana com lascas de bacalhua*, Alentejo soup with cods' tongues, then select from at least three bacalhau main dishes. If you're not a fan, meat dishes are also available. Portions are all huge so ask for a half portion or share. The trio of tables at this hole-in-the-wall, right over the river, are highly sought-after in summer.

ODE Port Wine House €€€€ *Largo do Terreiro 7; tel: 913 200 010; Tue–Sun 7–11pm, Fri and Sat 7pm–midnight* Fine dining in a romantic little restaurant with medieval stone walls, beams and candlelit tables. The emphasis is on slow food based on dishes cooked by the owner's grandmother and mother, and given a modern twist. Ingredients are sourced from local farmers using traditional methods and all the dishes are cooked in a small open-view kitchen. Cash only.

Traça €€ *Largo de São Domingos 88; tel: 222 081 065;* www.restaurantetraca.com; *Mon-Fri noon–11pm, Sat and Sun 12.30–11pm* Stylish restaurant in a 17th-century building serving authentic Iberian fare such as *salpicão de caça* (smoked sausage made from game), *maozinhas de porco* (pigs' trotters), *cabrito* (kid) and *polvo em Vinho do Porto e grelos* (octopus with port wine sauce and turnip tops). Slow food is the name of the game. For more conventional tastes there are crispy prawns, steaks and pork. Weekday lunchtime set menus are good value.

BAIXA

Caldeireiros € *Rua dos Caldeireiros 139; tel: 223 214 074; Mon–Sat 12.30–3.30pm, 6pm–1am* Bustling restaurant with communal tables and a good choice of *petiscos* (tapas). Try the *alheira de caça* (game sausage), *petingas* (tiny fish), grilled octopus salad, tripe Porto-style, salt-cod croquettes or steak.

Cantina 32 €€–€€€ *Rua das Flores 32; tel: 222 039 069; Mon-Sat 12.30–3pm, 6.30–11pm* Trendy restaurant on the attractive Rua das Flores, with industrial-chic setting, long communal tables and Portuguese specialities. Plenty of options for vegetarians.

Cantinho do Avillez €€€ *Rua Mouzinho da Silveira 166; tel: 223 227 879;* www.cantinhodoavillez.pt; *Mon-Fri 12.30–3pm, 7pm–midnight, Sat and Sun 12.30pm–midnight* Star chef José Avillez opened this restaurant in the centre of Porto following the success of his restaurants in Lisbon. Decor is cheerful and casual, the cuisine simple but sophisticated. Among his celebrated dishes are giant Algarve red shrimps with Thai flavours, flaked cod with bread crumbs, LT egg and 'exploding' olives and Barrosã PDO hamburger. For a dessert with a wow factor try the Hazelnut Trio.

Dama Pé de Cabra € *Passeio de São Lázaro 5; tel: 223 196 776; Tue-Sat 9.30am–3.30pm, Fri and Sat also 7.30–10pm* Small charming café 10

minutes' walk east of São Bento station, which makes a great spot for breakfast or brunch. Try the delicious flavoured breads (chestnut, pumpkin seed and carrot), homemade jams, scrambled eggs, superior sandwiches and lovely platter of cheese and cured meats.

DOP €€€€ *Palácio das Artes, Largo São Domingos 18; tel: 222 014 313; www.ruipaula.com; Tue–Sat 12.30–3pm, 7.30–11pm, Mon 12.30–3pm* Leading chef Rui Paula describes the dishes at his elegant restaurant within a palace as 'cheerful, colourful and fragrant'. Try octopus carpaccio with pomegranate or seabass ceviche followed perhaps by lobster and fish risotto or veal cheek with gnocchi. Two tasting menus, 'Memory' and 'Sea', both with wine pairing, are weekday lunch options.

Ernesto €€ *Rua da Picaria 85; tel: 222 002 600; www.oernesto.pt; Tue–Sat 8.30am–3.30pm, 6.30pm–midnight, Mon 8.30am–3.30pm* Established in 1938, this family restaurant is a favourite with locals for its authentic Portuguese fare such as *bacalhau* (cod), grilled octopus, tripe Porto-style, roast kid and veal. Friendly service and attractive setting with beams, stone walls and modern art.

Escondidinho Do Barredo € *Rua Canastreiros 28; tel: 222 057 229; Tue–Sun 9am–11pm* 'Escondidinho' means hidden, and hidden it really is. Don't look for the name, look for the red door. The simple homely *taberna* is run by two delightful sisters (who don't speak English) and has an open kitchen serving *petiscos* (tapas) for the more adventurous tastes: tripe, pigs' ears, octopus, as well as *bolinhos de bacalhau* (codfish cakes) and sardines, all of which can be washed down with amazingly cheap house wine. Very popular with locals and always busy.

Café Guarany €€€ *Avenida dos Aliados 85-89; tel: 223 321 272; www. cafeguarany.com; daily 9am–midnight* Under the same ownership as the famous Café Majestic (see page 111), Café Guarany serves the same pastries but at much cheaper prices, and also serves fish and meat dishes. On the main Avenida dos Aliados, this is a historical brasserie-style café, established in 1933 and traditionally a haunt of musicians. Expect live music and entertainment on Friday and Saturday nights.

Lado B Café € *Rua Passos Manuel 190/192; tel: 222 142 69; Mon–Thu 11am–11.30pm; Fri–Sat 11am–2am* On Rua Passos Manuel, Santiago (see above) is the most famous for *francesinha*, but Lado B, another basic diner, is pretty good too and rarely as crowded. You'll need to try both to see if you agree with their claim: *'A Melhor Francesinha do Mundo'* (The Best Francesinha in the World). Skip breakfast and come with a large appetite. Other options are burgers, steak sandwiches and salads.

Café Majestic €€ *Rua de Santa Catarina 112; tel: 222 003 887; www.cafe-majestic.com; Mon–Sat 9am–11.30pm* Dating back to 1921 and formerly a haunt of Porto's literati, this elegant café is today on every tourist's bucket list and there is nearly always a queue outside for a table. It's probably the most expensive café in Porto but the opulent Belle Époque interior – and the *rabanadas* (French toast with creamy egg custard) – are hard to resist.

Café Piolho € *Praça de Parada Leitão 45; tel: 222 003 749; Mon–Sat 7am–4am* Even though its official name is Café Âncora D'Ouro (and that's the name it has outside), everyone calls it Café Piolho. Dating from 1909, it is well known as a meeting place for students and teachers from the university nearby, and also for demos during the dictatorship. Very popular, particularly on Friday and Saturday evenings when students meet here for the first drink of the night.

Café Santiago € *Rua Passos Manuel 226; tel: 222 055 797; Mon–Sat noon–11pm* This basic café is renowned for Porto's speciality, the meat-filled multi-layered *francesinha*, covered in melted cheese, topped with a fried egg, drenched in a dark sauce and accompanied by chips if you wish. Be prepared for queues at weekends or go to the less crowded Lado B (see below).

MASSARELOS

Antiqvvm €€€€ *Rua de Entrequintas 220; tel: 226 000 445; www.antiqvvm. pt; Tue–Sat noon–midnight, Sun noon–3pm, Terrace open Sun 3–7pm* Enjoy Michelin-starred cuisine, fine wines and river views from this elegant restaurant beside the Museu Romántico. Chef Vitor Matos reinterprets traditional Portuguese cuisine, and each dish is artfully presented. Choose from the fixed-price lunch menu, tasting menus at €90 and €120 (with paired wines) or *à la carte*. A glassed-in gallery opens on to a large courtyard for alfresco dining in warm weather.

Rota do Chà € *Rua Miguel Bombarda 457; tel: 220 136 726; Mon–Sat 11am–8pm, Sun noon–8pm* A tea lover's haven, with an oriental vibe in the artsy Bombarda quarter. Choose from over 300 blends (staff are on hand if you're bamboozled) and sip tea in one of the tranquil spaces or the hidden garden, maybe with a slice of chocolate caramel pie or an apple muffin. Don't just pop in for a quick cuppa – everything is slow and mindful here, including the service.

VILA NOVA DE GAIA

Barão Fladgate €€€€ *Rua do Choupelo 250; tel: 223 772 951; www.barao-fladgate.com; daily 12.30–3pm, 7.30–10.30pm* Named after John Fladgate, a 19th-century Port shipper, Taylor's port wine lodge restaurant offers an elegant setting with glorious views across the Douro River to Porto as well as fine wining and dining. Ideally visit the Port Cellars first (see page 67) then lunch or dine at the restaurant. Set week-day lunches are good value.

Vinum Restaurant €€€€ *Graham's Port Lodge, Rua do Agro 141; tel: 220 930 417; daily 12.30–4pm, 6.30–11pm* A seductive spot combining dazzling views down to the river, the best dishes of the Douro, Trás-os-Montes, the Minho and the Atlantic and, of course, expert pairing with wines from the famous Graham's cellars. The menu features fish fresh from Matosinhos Market and rare Vaca Velha beef from Trás-os-Montes. Vinum also has a wine bar offering lighter meals and sharing plates.

The Yeatman €€€€ *Rua do Choupelo 88; tel: 220 122 100; daily 12.30–3pm, 7.30–11pm* Part of the famous Yeatman hotel, this is a favourite destination of wine lovers and gourmands. It is the only restaurant in Porto with two Michelin stars, offers perfect pairing of food and wine and has gorgeous views over Porto and the River Douro. Chef Ricardo Costa showcases the best of Portuguese products, laying emphasis on local produce and giving traditional dishes an innovative twist.

BEYOND PORTO

Leça da Palmeira

Casa de Chá da Boa Nova €€€€ *Avenida da Liberdade No 1681, Leça da Palmeira; tel: 229 940 066; www.casadechadaboanova.pt; Mon 7.30–11pm, Tue–Sat 12.30–3pm and 7.30–11pm* The tea house (casa de chà) is a National Monument: a seductive and sleek structure built into the rocks above the sea, designed by Portugal's leading architect Álvaro Siza Vieira. Choose from three tasting menus: Land and Sea, Atlantic or Boa Nova, with optional wine pairings, and be prepared for a hefty bill. Original and interesting combinations, such as eel and date foie gras or line-caught hake with plankton and barnacles earned Porto-born Chef Rui Paula a Michelin star in 2017. Reservations are essential.

Foz do Douro

Bocca €€–€€€ *Rua do Passeio Alegre 3, Foz do Douro; tel: 226 170 004; daily 12.30–11.30pm* This new glass box has a terrace and fabulous waterfront setting overlooking the River Douro. The food is Italian-inspired and the decor quite sophisticated and contemporary. Fish dishes include gambas, salmon ceviche, mussels in brandy and *corvina* with coriander rice; also delicious crusty pizzas from the wood-burning oven and an excellent choice of Portuguese wines.

Pedro Lemos €€€€ *Rua do Padre Luís Cabral 974, Foz do Douro; tel: 220 115 986; www.pedrolemos.net; Tue–Sat 12.30–3pm, 7.30–11pm* Hidden away on a street in the old town of Foz, Pedro Lemos' eponymous Michelin-star restaurant is a foodie haven, with exquisite dishes centring around set menus of five or seven courses, plus desserts.

Tavi € *Rua Senhora da Lux 363, Foz do Douro; tel: 226 180 152; daily 8.30am–8pm* Ocean views (if you can get a terrace seat) and fabulous

cakes and pastries lure tourists to Tavi. Good for breakfast or brunch and for watching the sun set over the Atlantic.

Matoshinos

Salta o Muro € *Rua Heróis de Franca 386, Matoshinos; tel: 229 380 870; www.saltaomuro.pt; Tue–Sat 12.15–3pm, 7–11pm* Typical of Matoshinos's fish restaurants this is a basic, bustling family-run place, packed with locals and tourists in the know. Favourite fish dishes are octopus with rice, *caldeirada* (fish soup), sardines and turbot – all simply cooked, fresh and delicious. Not much English is spoken but there's a list with fish translated into English. Excellent value.

Esplanada Marisqueira A Antiga €€€€ *Rua Roberto Ivens 628, Matosinhos; tel: 229 380 660; www.esplanadamarisqueira.com; daily noon–1am* If you want to splash out on a gourmet fish restaurant this is the place to go. It serves some of the best seafood in Porto and the seafood platter is to die for. Booking advised.

A-Z TRAVEL TIPS

A SUMMARY OF PRACTICAL INFORMATION

A

ACCOMMODATION

The most appealing places to stay are found in the city centre, while the newer, more bland hotels (many with business facilities) are further out of town, for example at Boavista. Here you get more for your euros but the sheer convenience of being near the centre, in a city of hills, is worth a lot. The hotel scene has been burgeoning in recent years with the opening of dozens of new hotels, many of them upmarket or chic boutique hotels. The city has also seen a surge of Airbnbs, apartments and guest houses. Prices are steadily increasing but Porto is still good value compared with most cities in western Europe.

In high season (June–September) rooms are at a premium and you should book well ahead. Spring and late autumn are busy periods too, but in mid-winter Porto is relatively peaceful and prices can fall substantially. Whatever time you visit the best rates are usually secured by booking in advance. If you arrive on spec, head for one of the tourist offices (see page 130) who will help you find accommodation. The official tourist board website (www.visitportoandnorth.travel) features an accommodation section with hotels ranging from 5 to 2-star.

Many hotels charge extra for breakfast. Check when you make a reservation. Charges can be high (eg €18 per person in a 4-star hotel) and you may prefer to go to the local café for coffee and croissants at a fraction of the price.

Be prepared for the City Tourist Tax, introduced in 2018 for those staying overnight in the city. The charge is €2 per adult per night, subject to a maximum of seven nights, but not applicable to children under 14. The tax is not included in the rates advertised on hotel booking websites and is charged directly to guests at the hotel.

What's the rate per night? **Qual é o preço por noite?**

AIRPORT

Porto's **Aeroporto Francisco Sá Carneiro** (www.ana.pt) is 17km (10.5 miles) north of the city centre. The easiest way to get to the centre of Porto is by Metro Purple Line E in the direction of Estádio do Dragão, changing at Casa da Música (which serves Boavista hotels) on to the yellow Trindade Line D for central hotels. The metro runs from 6am–1am, there are two or three trains an hour and the journey takes 35–45 minutes. The multi-option metro ticket machines can be a bit complex for first-timers but there is a good tourist office at the airport which sells tickets. Taxis to the centre cost €20–35.

> How much is it to downtown Porto? **Quanto custa para ir ao centro de Porto?**

B

BICYCLE HIRE

Given Porto's hilly terrain, uneven streets and traffic-filled lanes, few tourists choose to hire a bike, or if they do it's an electric one. However there is easy biking along a cycle path all the way from the Dom Luís I bridge alongside the River Douro to the beaches of Foz do Douro and extending to Matosinhos. Across the river in Vila Nova de Gaia you can also cycle beside the river, then south via the Reserva Natural Local do Estuário do Douro (nature reserve) to the beaches of Espinho. In Ribeira bikes can be rented from Porto Rent a Bike, Avenida Gustavo Eiffel No. 280 (www.portorentabike.com) on the waterfront, just beyond the Dom Luís I bridge. Electric, tandem and folding bikes are available, and accessories such as locks, maps, helmets and child seats are included in the price. A Dutch bike costs €10 for half a day, €15 for 24 hours.

BUDGETING FOR YOUR TRIP

Accommodation. A double room in a simple hotel or B&B costs €80–120, in the mid-range category from €120–180 and for a 4-star plus expect to pay over €200. Hostel accommodation is plentiful, with dorms for around €20 and double rooms from €40–75.

Flights. Flights from London airports start at around £65 return off season, with a low-cost carrier. Summer flights are more likely to be £200–300.

Meals and drinks. Eating out is more affordable than most European capitals, especially if you choose to have your main meal at lunchtime. A 3-course dinner with wine in a mid-range restaurant would cost around €30 or in an upmarket one from €40 upwards. Portions are often gargantuan and you can cut costs by sharing. Most restaurants offer a midday fixed-price meal, often no more than €10–15 for three courses. A coffee costs anything from 70 cents (espresso in a local bar) to €3 (cappuccino served in a smart bar or main square); local beer is €1.50–3, a bottle of wine in a restaurant €10–20, house wine in a carafe a good deal less.

Museums. Admission fees range from €2.50–10. Some museums are free on the first Sunday of the month, others (eg Serralves Museum of Contemporary Art and Soares dos Reis National Museum) are free on Sundays until 1pm.

The Porto Card includes free admission to 11 museums and a 50% discount on eight sights, plus an optional travel card for unlimited access to the metro, buses and urban trains. Cards are available online and at the airport (purchase it there to save on travel to the centre). The hour and date should be written on the back of your card when you first use it. A card without transport costs €6, €10, €13 and €15 for 1, 2, 3 and 4 days, passes with travel for the same periods are €13, €20, €25 and €33.

C

CAMPING

There is no camping in Porto itself and the nearest sites are around a 50–60-minute bus journey away from the city centre. The chain Orbitur (www.orbitur.pt) has two sites, Orbitur Angeiras 16km (10 miles) north of Porto at the seaside village of Angeiras, and Orbitur Madalena, close to Madalena beach, 8km (5 miles) from the centre of Vila Nova de Gaia. Campsites in the region tend to be very crowded and noisy in summer.

CAR HIRE

Major international companies such as Avis, Hertz and Europcar have offices both at the airport and in Porto, but for the best deals book online in advance. Local companies include Auto-Jardim (www.auto-jardimrentacar.pt) and Bluealliance (www.bluealliance.pt). Car rental costs from around €150 per week for a small car. The minimum age of hiring a car is 21–25 (depending on the company) and anyone hiring must have held a valid licence for at least one year. Rental companies will accept your home country's national driving license but you must show your passport. Third-party insurance should be included in the basic charge. Optional excess insurance costs from around €15 a day; it is far cheaper to take out your own excess insurance policy in advance.

I'd like to rent a car for one day/week **Queria alugar um carro por um dia/uma semana**

CLIMATE

July and August are the hottest months, although there are rarely heat waves. June, September and October are warm, pleasant and less crowded. Porto is well north of Lisbon and has far more rain. The wettest months are October to January, but April can be wet too and late spring can be surprisingly cool. Winter is the quietest (and coldest) season, with some great hotel discounts. In the Douro Valley the summers are stifling and should be avoided. If you want to witness (or even join in) the grape harvest, go from mid to late September, but for the colours of the foliage wait until late October or early November.

	J	F	M	A	M	J	J	A	S	O	N	D
C	10	11	12	13	15	18	20	20	19	16	13	12
F	50	52	54	55	59	64	68	68	66	61	55	54

CLOTHING

Apart from the mid-summer months, when all you need is light, cool clothes and perhaps a wrap or sweater, bring plenty of layers, an umbrella and raincoat and in winter a warm coat or anorak. A pair of comfortable walking shoes is essential for the steep and cobbled streets. When visiting churches cover shoulders and don't wear skimpy attire.

CRIME AND SAFETY

Take precautions against pickpockets – and beware that some of them don smart attire to avoid suspicion. Leave important documents and valuables in the hotel safe and keep a firm hold of handbags, especially in crowded public areas and on public transport. For insurance purposes theft and loss must be reported immediately to the police (see below under Emergencies).

D

DISABLED TRAVELLERS

Porto's cobbled streets and steep hills don't make it easy for disabled travellers, but several of the main attractions are accessible. Most of the metro is accessible, as are some buses, but trams are inaccessible. Taxis are often the best option – drivers tend to be helpful and friendly and the prices are low. Adapted & Senior Tours Portugal (www.adaptedtoursportugal.com) offer holidays catered to people with disabilities. For more information on accessible tourism in Portugal visit https://www.visitportugal.com/en/experiencias/turismo-acessivel.

DRIVING

Avoid driving in the city centre if at all possible. Roads are congested and parking expensive. Most visitors cover Porto on foot, or use buses, trams, the metro or the affordable taxis and Ubers. Few tourists find it necessary to hire a car to see the region, but driving is one of the best ways of seeing the Douro valley (see page 81).

To bring your own car into Portugal you will need your national driving licence, registration papers and insurance. The main roads are generally in good repair.

Rules and regulations. The rules of the road are the same as in most western European countries. Drive on the right. At roundabouts the vehicle already on the roundabout has priority unless road markings or lights indicate otherwise. Seat belts are compulsory and a heavy fine can be imposed for not wearing one. Speed limits are 120km/h (75mph) on motorways, 100km/h (62.5mph) on roads restricted to motor vehicles, 90km/h (56mph) on other roads and 50km/h (37mph) in urban areas.

Breakdowns. Dial 112 for an operator to connect you to an emergency service. Operators can answer your call in English.

Are we on the right road for...? **É esta estrada para...?**
Fill the tank, please **Encha o depósito faz favor**
My car's broken down **O meu carro está avariado**
There's been an accident **Houve um acidente**

E

ELECTRICITY

220V/50Hz is standard. Sockets take two-pin, round pronged plugs. Visitors from the UK and the US will require an adaptor or transformer.

EMBASSIES AND CONSULATES

Australia Avenida da Liberdade 200, 2nd floor, Lisbon, tel: (+351) 213 101 500; https://portugal.embassy.gov.au/

Canada Avenida da Liberdade 198-200, 3rd floor, Lisbon, tel: (+351) 213 164 600; www.canadainternational.gc.ca/portugal/

Ireland Avenida da Liberdade 200, 4th floor, Lisbon, tel: (+351) 213 308 200; www.dfa.ie/irish-embassy/portugal/

New Zealand Rua de Sociedade Farmacêutica 68, Lisbon, tel: (+351) 213 140 780; https://www.mfat.govt.nz/

South Africa Avenida Luís Bivar 10, Lisbon, tel: (+351) 213 192 200; www.embaixada-africadosul.pt

UK Rua de São Bernardo 33, Lisbon, tel: (+351) 213 924 000; https://www.gov.uk/world/organisations/british-embassy-lisbon

US Avenida das Forças Armadas 16, Lisbon, tel: (+351) 217 273 300; https://pt.usembassy.gov/

Where's the British/American embassy? **Onde é a embaixada inglesa/americana?**

EMERGENCIES

General emergency, 24 hours a day: 112

G

GETTING THERE

By air. Porto is linked by daily direct flights with many European cities. Portugal's flag carrier airline, TAP Air Portugal (www.flytap.com) and British Airways (www.ba.com) operate scheduled flights between London and Porto. The city is also well served by low-cost UK carriers including Ryanair (www.ryanair.com) and easyJet (www.easyjet.com).

TAP Air Portugal and United Airlines (www.united.com) both operate direct services to Porto from New York; Air Transat (www.airtransat.com) and Air Canada (www.aircanada.com) fly direct from Toronto to Porto.

By Sea. Cruise ships dock at Leixões, about 10km (just over 6 miles) from the centre of Porto. Brittany Ferries (www.brittany-ferries.co.uk) have crossings from Portsmouth, UK to Santander and Bilbao in Spain and from Plymouth to Santander. The drive from northern Spain to Porto is then likely to take another 6–7 hours.

By rail. Portugal is linked to the European railway network and connections to Porto are possible from points throughout Spain, France and the rest of continental Europe. The Portuguese national railway network is called CP (Comboios de Portugal, www.cp.pt). The main railway station in Porto is Campanhã, where international, national and regional trains arrive. From here there are regular connections to the central city station of São Bento.

By car. Major motorways connect Portugal with Spain at numerous border points. The drive from London to Porto via France and Spain takes 21–23 hours (1,259 miles/2026km). Porto and Lisbon are linked by the A1, with a journey time of around three hours. France, Spain and Portugal all charge highway tolls.

GUIDES AND TOURS

Information on tours is available at tourist offices or from your hotel. River trips depart from the quaysides on both sides of the River Douro. Several different companies offer the hour-long, scenic Six Bridges cruise (€12–15 per person), some offering the option of combining it with a visit to port wine cellars. Living Tours (www.livingtours.com) offer a wide choice of well-run guided tours in Porto and beyond, including Douro Valley cruises. For something a bit different, try At Will Tours (www.atwilltours.com), who offer personalised tours with themes such as 'Live like a Local' or 'Street Art'. And for a food theme look no further than Taste Porto Food and Wine Tours (www.tasteporto.com). Simply B Free (www.freetoursporto.com, tel: 933 501 007) offer free 3-hour walking tours of Porto daily in English and Spanish at 10.15am and 3.15pm. These are easy-going, friendly tours for all ages with a maximum of 10 people. You can turn up at the starting point, São Bento railway station, just before the start of the walk, but to be sure of securing a place it's best to email or telephone in advance.

Various companies offer hop-on, hop-off bus tours with open-top buses and in season a tourist train loops around the centre and crosses the river for a stop at Vila Nova de Gaia.

> We'd like an English-speaking guide **Queremos um guia que fale inglês**

H

HEALTH AND MEDICAL CARE

Standards of hygiene in Porto and in Portugal as a whole are generally very high; the most likely illness to befall travellers will be the result of an excess of sun or alcohol. The water is safe to drink. Farmácias (chemists/drugstores) are open during normal business hours and one shop in each neighbourhood is on duty around the clock. Addresses can be found on pharmacy doors or in the daily paper, *Jornal de Notícias*. The main hospital in Porto is the Hospital Santo António, Largo do Prof Abel Salazar, tel: 222 077 500, open 24 hours. In the event of an accident or sudden illness, call 112. There is no charge and the number is accessible from anywhere in the country at any time of day. Check your medical insurance to be sure it covers illness or accident while you are abroad. EU nationals with a European Health Insurance card (EHIC) obtained before departure (at www.ehic.org.uk in the UK) can receive free emergency treatment at Social Security and municipal hospitals in Portugal. Privately billed hospital visits are expensive. UK residents should be aware that current arrangements may be affected by Brexit.

Where's the nearest (all night) pharmacy? **Onde fica a farmácia (de serviço) mais próxima?**
I need a doctor/dentist **Preciso de um médico/dentista**
an ambulance **uma ambulância**

L

LANGUAGE

Portuguese is the sixth most spoken language in the world, with around 220 million native speakers and 260 million total speakers. It is spoken in Brazil, Angola, Mozambique and Macau – all former colonies of Portugal. Any school Spanish may help with signs and menus, but will not unlock the mysteries of spoken Portuguese with its many nasal sounds. Virtually all hotels have staff who speak English and unless you go off the beaten track you should have little problem communicating in shops or restaurants. Most menus are translated into English; if not waiters will assist. The older taxi drivers may not speak English, but if you write down the destination this should not be a problem. Almost everyone understands Spanish and many speak French, particularly the older generation, but just learning a few simple words and phrases in Portuguese will certainly enhance your visit and help if you are off the tourist circuit.

LGBTQ TRAVELLERS

Porto is becoming one of the most popular gay tourist destinations in Europe. It may be a little more conservative than Amsterdam or Berlin, but attitudes are generally relaxed and you will see plenty of same-sex couples wandering the city streets. The Porto Pride party held here in July each year first took place in 2001. Now the city also hosts the Porto International Queer Film Festival in October. For local information on gay life in Porto visit www.portogaycircuit.com. Bars and clubs catering for an LGBTQ crowd are plentiful. Popular venues are Pride Café (Praça

Marquês de Pombal 13), a gay café by day and dance floor by night, Zoom Nightclub (Rua de Passos Manuel 40, Fri and Sat only) and Invictus (Rua da Conceição 8/9), a small café/bar with drag shows.

M

MAPS

Tourist information offices and hotels provide free maps of Porto and the surrounding area, though it's hard to find one with all the small streets marked.

MEDIA

Europe's principal newspapers, including most British dailies, are available on the day of publication. The weekly *Portugal News* (www.theportugalnews.com), published in the Algarve, is the country's main English-language paper and covers news and stories from around the country. Free Portuguese/English booklets include *Lisboa Convida* (also online at www.lisboa.convida.pt), a six-monthly shopping and leisure guide, available from tourist offices and some hotels. Many but by no means all hotels have TVs with English-language channels such as BBC News and CNN. Foreign films are usually shown in the original language with subtitles.

MONEY MATTERS

Currency. In common with most other European countries, the official currency used in Portugal is the euro (€), divided into 100 cents. Euro notes come in denominations of 500, 200, 100, 50, 20, 10 and 5; coins come in denominations of 2 and 1, then 50, 20, 10, 5, 2 and 1 cents.

Credit cards and cash machines. MasterCard and Visa are the most widely accepted credit cards. Many places don't accept American Express. Some small shops and restaurants are cash only, or take credit cards only for purchases of more than €10. You also need to have cash handy for museums and nightclubs. Cash machines are widespread. You can take out a maximum of €200 a day.

Exchange facilities. Banks offer the best rates, followed by exchange offices and hotels. Some exchange offices offer commission-free facilities, but check that the exchange rate is not exorbitant.

Can I pay with a credit card? **Posso pagar com cartão de crédito?**
How much is that? **Quanto custa isto?**
Where's the nearest bank/currency exchange office? **Onde fica o banco mais próximo/a casa de câmbio mais próxima?**

O

OPENING HOURS

Banks open Mon–Fri 8.30am–3pm. Shops open Mon–Sat 9.30/10am–7/7.30pm, although some have shorter opening hours on Saturday and some of the smaller shops close for lunch. An increasing number of outlets are now open on Sundays, including shopping centres outside the city centre. Many shops and galleries in the Bombarda district don't open until noon, closing at 7 or 8pm.

Most museums are closed on Monday and public holidays.

P

POLICE

The Portuguese national police, identified by their blue uniforms, are generally helpful and often speak a little English. On the roads, traffic is controlled by the Guarda Nacional Republicana (GNR). Occasionally police make spot-checks on documents or tyres and can issue on-the-spot fines, payable in cash only.

The multilingual Tourist Police are at Rua Clube dos Fenianos 11 (tel: 222 081 833; daily 8am–2am) beside the main tourist office.

The general emergency number is 112.

> Where's the nearest police station? **Onde fica o posto de polícia mais próximo?**
> I've lost my ...wallet/bag/passport **Perdi...a minha carteira/o meu saco/o meu passaporte**

POST OFFICES

Post offices (*correios*) are normally open Mon–Fri 9am–6pm but the main post office, the Posto de Correios dos Aliados on Praça General Humberto Delgado, has longer hours: Mon–Fri 8.30am–9pm, Sat 9am–6pm.

> Where's the nearest post office? **Onde fica a estação de correios mais próxima?**

PUBLIC HOLIDAYS

1 January *Ano Novo* New Year's Day
25 April *Dia da Liberdade* 1974 Revolution Day
1 May *Dia do Trabalhador* May Day
10 June *Dia de Portugal* or *Dia de Camões* National Day
24 June *São João* (Porto only)
15 August *Assunção* The Assumption
5 October *Implantação da República* Republic Day
1 November *Todos-os-Santos* All Saints' Day
1 December *Dia da Independência* Independence Day
8 December *Imaculada Conceição* Immaculate Conception
25 December *Natal* Christmas Day
Moveable dates:

Sexta-feira Santa Good Friday
Corpo de Deus Corpus Christi

R

RELIGION

The Portuguese are predominantly Roman Catholic, a fact reflected in surviving religious rituals and saints' days that are public holidays. However only a small percentage regularly attend Mass. The St James Anglican Church Porto on Largo da Maternidade de Julio Dinis (www. stjamesoporto.org) holds services on Sundays and Thursdays.

T

TELEPHONES

Portugal's country code is 351. The local area code for Porto is 22 and must be dialled before all phone numbers, including local calls. To make an international call, dial 00 followed by the country code (UK 44, Australia 61, Canada and the US 1), plus the phone number including the area code, but without the initial '0' where there is one.

Mobile (cell) phones. Check the international roaming rates with your provider prior to departure. In mid-2017 roaming charges within the EU were abolished (but could be reintroduced for UK citizens post-Brexit). Roaming charges can be quite high for non-EU countries and if you are making a lot of calls or staying for some time it may be worth purchasing a SIM 'pay as you go' card available at shops of the main providers or at the post office.

TIME ZONES

Portugal, being at the western edge of Europe, maintains Greenwich Mean Time (GMT), along with the UK, and is therefore one hour behind the rest of the EU. From the last Sunday in March until the last Sunday in October the clocks are moved one hour ahead for summer time, GMT + 1.

New York	London	**Porto**	Paris	Sydney	Auckland
7am	noon	**noon**	1pm	9pm	11pm

TIPPING

Service is not usually added to restaurant bills and a tip of 10% is normal, provided you think the service warrants it. Hotel porters generally receive a euro for each bag they carry; taxi drivers don't necessarily expect a tip but are grateful if you round the fare up.

TOILETS

Public toilets are hard to come by, but you can find them in stations, museums and large shops. Otherwise it is generally a case of using the facilities of a café or bar. Toilets are marked *Senhoras* (ladies) and *Homens* (men).

Where are the toilets? **Onde é o lavabo/quarto de banho?**

TOURIST INFORMATION

Tourist offices can provide a free city map, list of opening hours for city sights and a programme of current events. There are two main tourist offices: **Turismo Central** at Rua Clube dos Fenianos 25, at the top of Avenida dos Aliados, tel: 223 393 472 (daily Nov–May 9am–7pm, June–Oct 9am–8pm and Aug until 9pm) and **Turismo Sé** at Terreiro da Sé, occupying the medieval tower opposite the Cathedral, tel: 223 393 472 (same opening hours). Other tourist offices and information offices:

Porto's **Francisco Sá Carneiro airport** has a good tourist office in the Arrivals Hall.

iPoint Aliados, green kiosk on Praça da Liberdade (May–Oct daily 9.30am–6.30pm, Nov–Apr weather permitting Mon–Fri 9.30am–7pm).

iPoint Campanhã, inside Campanhã railway station (daily June–Aug 9.30am–6.30pm with one hour break).

iPoint Ribeira Praça da Ribeira (daily May–Sept 10.30am–7pm, Oct 10.30am–6pm).

Vila Nova de Gaia Turismo on the waterfront at Avenida Diogo Leite 135, tel: 223 758 288 (Apr–Sept daily 10am–6pm, Oct–Mar Mon–Sat 10am–6pm).

TRANSPORT

Metro. Porto has a swish modern metro system (www.metrodoporto. pt) operating six easy-to-use lines, A to F. Trains run from 6am–1am, and arrive every 4–15 minutes. The network is limited and for visitors the most useful routes are Line E (Purple) between the airport and the centre, Line A (Blue) linking Porto to Matosinhos and Line B (Red) to the seaside resort of Vila do Conde. All lines converge at the Trindade stop, just north of Avenida dos Aliados. For getting around the centre you are better off going by foot, bus or tram, though the Casa da Música metro stop is useful if you are staying in Boavista or visiting the concert hall or Serralves. Currently in progress is a new Line G (Pink) which will link Casa da Música and São Bento via Plaza de Galicia and Hospital de Santo António; and in Vila Nova de Gaia Line D (Yellow) is being extended by 3.2km (2 miles).

Rechargeable Andante cards can be used for the metro, buses and some suburban trains. (Trams, funiculars, boats and cable-car have different tickets and prices.) The card cost is €0.60 and is available from ticket machines, Andante shops (eg in the airport and metro stations) and also from railway stations, tourist offices and some hotels. The card can be credited for single journeys, 10 tickets or 24-hour travel. The price depends on which of the three zones (Z2, Z3 and Z4) you travel to. Zone 2 is sufficient for getting around central Porto but the airport is in Zone 4. One trip for Zone 2 costs €1.20, for Zone 4 it is €1.85. Transfers can be made within one hour with the same ticket. If you change metro lines you have to swipe your card again. One and three day travel cards with unlimited travel on the metro, buses and locals trains are available. Cards are activated when first used and must be validated on each journey. The metro is open from 6am–1am.

> Where can I get a taxi? **Onde posso encontrar um táxi?**
> What's the fare to...? **Quanto custa um bilhete para...?**
> Where is the nearest bus stop? **Onde é a paragem de autocarros mais próxima?**
> I want a ticket to... **Queria um bilhete para...**
> single/return **ida/ida e volta**
> Will you tell me when to get off? **Pode dizer-me quando devo descer?**

Trains. Trains are run by CP (Comboios de Portugal, www.cp.pt). The main railway station in Porto is the Estação de Campanhã, on the east edge of town, where international and national trains on longer routes (eg from Lisbon) arrive. The station and the area are to undergo a €40 million overhaul from 2019–2021. From Campanhã station there are constant connections to the Estação de São Bento, the central railway station used for most of the regional and inter-regional services. Both Campanhã and São Bento have metro stations. Timetables and fares are available on the CP website. Discounts on train journeys are available for those with a student card or who are under 26.

Bus and tram. Porto has an extensive bus system operated by STCP (www.stcp.pt). Main hubs are Jardim da Cordoaria, Praça Almeida Garrett and Praça da Liberdade. You can buy a ticket on board or use an Andante card (see above). Tickets must be validated in the machine on the bus. Information on fares and timetables is available on the STCP website. Buses usually operate between 6am and midnight or 1am. The most scenic route is bus No. 500 which links the centre of Porto to Foz do Douro.

The appealing vintage trams (carros eléctricos) only operate on three routes, the most popular (and crowded) being No. 1, which runs from the historic centre of Porto along the riverside to the coast. Trams are not covered by the Andante card. Tickets (€3 per journey) can be bought from the driver. The trams are hugely popular with tourists but locals tend to take the faster and cheaper buses. Tram times vary according to the time of year.

Funiculars. The useful Funicular dos Guindais connects the Ribeira, at the foot of the Dom Luís I bridge, with the city centre, climbing a steep hill to Rua da Batalha. Funiculars run every 10 minutes and tickets cost €2.50 each way. At Vila Nova de Gaia the panoramic Teleférico de Gaia cable car (www.gaiacablecar.com) climbs from the riverfront up to the Jardim do Morro. It's a pricey 5-minute ride (€6 one way, €9 return) but affords fine views of the wine lodges and Porto.

Taxis and tuk-tuks. Taxis in Porto are cheap by European standards. The cars are beige or black with a green roof. Taxi ranks can be found at main squares and stations but can also be hailed in the street. The fare is shown on the meter – check that it's running before you set off. There are extra charges at night and at weekends, and for luggage placed in the boot. For a radio taxi call Taxis Invicta (tel: 225 076 400) or Raditáxis (tel: 225 073 900). Uber works well in Porto and the fares are a good deal cheaper than those of normal taxis. Drivers normally turn up promptly. Water taxis link the waterfront at Ribeira with Vila Nova de Gaia opposite (€3 one way). Tuk-tuks, seating up to three, can be found at the most popular sights. Guided tours cost €15–65 depending on the length of the journey.

V

VISAS AND ENTRY REQUIREMENTS

For EU citizens, a valid passport or identity card is all that is needed to enter Portugal for stays of up to 90 days. Citizens of Australia, Canada,

New Zealand and the US require only a valid passport. For stays of more than 90 days a visa or residence permit is required.

W

WEBSITES AND INTERNET ACCESS

www.visitportoandnorth.travel Official tourist website for Porto and northern Portugal
www.visitportugal.com The official Portuguese tourism site
www.flytap.com TAP/Air Portugal, the national airline
www.cp.pt Comboios de Portugal, the railway network
Free Wi-Fi can be found in most cafés, bars, restaurants and hotels.

Y

YOUTH HOSTELS

Porto now has dozens of youth hostels spread around the city, ranging from very basic to luxury, with en suite double rooms. Some of the hostels organise activities such as free walks, theme nights and parties. Breakfast is often included in the room rate. At the very top of the list is the comfortable, art-themed Gallery Hostel Porto (see page 139). The centrally located Poets' Inn (Rua dos Caldeireiros 261, tel: 223 324 209, www.thepoetsinn.com), close to the Clérigos Tower, is newly furnished and tastefully decorated.

RECOMMENDED HOTELS

Porto now offers accommodation to suit all tastes: 5-star laps of luxury, chic boutique hotels, simple guest houses, hostels, apartments and Airbnbs. There's even a castle you can stay in. In high season (June to September) rooms are at a premium and you should book well ahead. The rates can change significantly with demand and facilities. Best rates are normally those booked through a hotel's own website. Discounts are sometimes available for stays of longer than three nights. Short-term rentals are becoming increasingly popular, but expect a minimum night stay.

The price indication is for a double room in high season including breakfast, service and VAT, but excluding the City Tourist Tax, which is €2 per person per night for visitors aged 14 and over (see page 116). All the hotels take major credit cards unless otherwise stated.

€€€€	over 250 euros
€€€	180–250 euros
€€	120–180 euros
€	under 120 euros

RIBEIRA

1872 River House €€€ *Rua do Infante D. Henrique; tel: 961 172 805;* www.1872riverhouse.com. A little gem of a hotel converted from a riverside townhouse. The eight individually furnished rooms face the city or river. Guests are very well looked after with excellent breakfasts (cold buffet with freshly made pastries and eggs to order) and welcoming, helpful staff. Tea, coffee, snacks and (unusually) beer are available all day.

Da Bolsa €€ *Rua Ferreira Borges 101; tel: 222 026 768;* www.hoteldabolsa.com. Three-star hotel in prime location in the heart of Porto, built in 1908 as a private social club, then rebuilt as the HQ of an insurance company. It is clean and comfortable with helpful staff, but bedrooms are a tad old-fashioned.

Guest House Douro €€-€€€ *Rua Fonte Taurina 99-101; tel: 222 015 135;* www.guesthousedouro.com. This was the first guest house on the Ribeira waterfront. A brave young couple, Carmen and João, bought and restored the house several years ago when Porto was rough around the edges and the city saw few tourists. Now their stylish rooms are very much in demand, with four of their eight rooms having direct views of the River Douro.

Infante Sagres €€€€ *Praça D. Filipa de Lencastre 62; tel: 223 398 500;* www.infantesagres.com. The *grande dame* of Porto's hotels reopened in 2018 after a major renovation. Among its VIPs have been the Dalai Lama and Bob Dylan as well as European royalty and presidents. Old-word elegance predominates, though new additions such as the Vogue Café with 'Food for the Fashionable' have added a touch of 21st-century glamour.

InPátio Guest House € *Pátio de São Salvador 22; tel: 351 934 448;* www. inpatio.pt. This is a centrally located but quiet B&B with stylish rooms. Owners Fernando and Olga extend a warm welcome and are happy to help organise your itinerary. Excellent breakfasts, with homemade bread and cake.

Pestana Vintage Port Hotel €€€€ *Praça da Ribeira 1; tel: 223 402 300;* www.pestana.com. A conversion of a group of old riverside houses, this pricey boutique hotel in the Pestana group has a prime location in the heart of Ribeira. Guest rooms are sleekly modern and comfortable but vary in shape and size. Many have superb views of the Dom Luís I bridge and river. Good half-board deals with lunch or dinner in the Rib Beef and Wine Restaurant.

Port River Apartments €€€ *Rua dos Canastreiros 50; tel: 223 401 210;* www.portoriver.pt. In a historic building in Ribeira, this apar-thotel is a stylish fusion of old and new. Rooms have rough stone walls, wood floors, exposed beams, contemporary furnishings and well-equipped kitchenettes. The best have views of the River Douro.

BAIXA (DOWNTOWN)

A.S.1829 €€ *Largo de São Domingos 45-55; tel: 223 402 740;* http://as1829.luxhotels.pt. The A.S. stands for Aranjo e Sobinho, a print business and stationery shop (dating from 1829) which once occupied the building. A small stationery shop still exists in the foyer. The hotel has a great location, just a short walk up from Ribeira. The rooms are stylish, comfy and contemporary, with double-glazing, and there is a great choice of restaurants within a stone's throw. The hotel's own Galeria do Largo restaurant, overlooking the square, serves up Portuguese traditional fare.

Cale Guest House € *Largo de São Domingos 28; tel: 966 686 081.* Popular little guest house in a perfect location a couple of minutes up from the waterfront. The seven newly furnished rooms have white walls, wood flooring and balcony or patio. Good breakfasts too, which are included in the room rate.

Casa dos Lóios €€ *Rua das Flores 245; tel: 914 176 969;* https://shiadu.com/en/cities/porto-en/. A charming and quirky guest house in an excellent location on the lovely Rua das Flores with very reasonable prices. It occupies part of a restored historic house and preserves some of the architectural features. The staff are exceptionally helpful, the breakfasts are good and there is complimentary tea, coffee and cake.

Castelo de Santa Catarina €€ *Rua de Santa Catarina 1347; tel: 225 095 599;* www.castelosantacatarina.com. If you don't mind being a little out of the centre, you can stay in a turreted castle surrounded by gardens. It dates from 1887 and was a private home before becoming a hotel. Accommodation is either in traditional rooms with period furnishings within the castle (NB no lift) or modern ones in the new wing.

Dom Henrique €€€ *Rua Guedes de Azevedo 179; tel: 223 401 616;* www.hoteldomhenrique.pt. This high-rise hotel north of the centre is geared to business travellers, but is also popular with tourists for its reasonable prices, spacious comfortable rooms, 4-star amenities and 17th-floor panoramic restaurant.

Grande Hotel de Paris €€ *Rua da Fábrica 27; tel: 222 073 140;* www.hotelparis.pt. A building long associated with music and literature, this became a hotel under French owners in 1877. 'Grand' is a tad misleading, but it has old-world charm, with small salons for reading and a fine breakfast room overlooking a garden of lemon trees and bird-of-paradise plants. Bedrooms and bathrooms could do with an update but given the location the prices are good.

InterContinental Porto €€€€ *Praça da Liberdade 25; tel: 220 035 600;* www.ihg.com. The historic Palácio das Cardosas, once the site of a monastery, now offers 5-star luxury and impeccable service. Right in the centre, it stands conspicuously at the southern end of the main Avenida dos Aliados, within easy walking distance of all the main sights. Inside it's plush and palatial with large chandeliers, marble floors and a gallery of exclusive shops. Guests can enjoy fine dining and expert wine pairing in the Astoria restaurant, and tea, cocktails and live-music in the elegant library-style Bar das Cardosas.

M Maison Particulière €€€ *Largo de São Domingos 66; tel: 227 661 400;* www.m-porto.com. Exclusive, French-inspired boutique hotel within a beautifully restored building, preserving stuccowork, wood-carved ceilings and original fireplaces. There are 10 individually designed suites, decorated with original antiques, luxury fabrics in warm tones and lithographs by famous modern artists. The location couldn't be better, close to the Ribeira waterfront, with an excellent choice of restaurants all around.

Poets' Inn € *Rua dos Caldeireiros 261; tel: 223 324 209;* www.thepoetsinn.com. This hostel is tucked down a quiet street, within walking distance of major landmarks and plentiful restaurants. It offers imaginatively decorated, comfortable rooms with shared bathrooms, friendly staff and a well-equipped kitchen.

São Domingos Oporto Tourist Apartments €€ *Largo São Domingos 86; tel: 915 161 181;* www.oportotouristapartments.com. Attractive contemporary apartments in an old building with high ceilings, wood floors and shutters. The location is perfect, just up from the Ribeira waterfront, and with such a good choice of neighbouring restaurants you may find the kichenette is superfluous. Good value.

Teatro €€€ *Rua Sá da Bandiera 84; tel: 220 409 620;* www.hotelteatro.pt. On the site of Porto's old Baquet Theatre, the hotel lives up to its name from the moment you arrive and collect your room ticket from the Box Office reception. Expect to come across elaborate costumes and dark, mysterious rooms with spotlights. Decor is plush, with black and gold predominating.

MIRAGAIA AND MASSARELOS

Gallery Hostel Porto € *Rua de Miguel Bombarda 222; tel: 224 964 313;* www.gallery-hostel.com. This hip hostel is ideal for art-lovers, occupying a 1906 townhouse packed with original works of art and located in the happening Bombarda arts quarter. Modern stylish en-suite dormitories, double rooms and suites are all art-themed; there's also a summer terrace, winter garden, changing art exhibitions and nightly Portuguese dinners. Free walking tours, free breakfast and free Wi-Fi, very friendly staff too. No wonder it's popular.

Mercador Guest House €€ *Rua de Miguel Bombarda 382; tel: 911 059 755;* http://porto.mercador.com.pt. Delightful quiet guest house with old-fashioned charm. Plus points are the garden, excellent breakfast, friendly helpful staff and a warm welcome with coffee and port on arrival. Peaceful TV-free guest rooms, most with balconies.

Pensão Favorita € *Rua de Miguel Bombarda 267; tel: 220 134 157;* www.pensaofavorita.pt. Charming guest house with a pretty and unexpected garden. There are seven rooms in the main house, five in the garden, in contemporary and vintage style, all with private bathroom. Very welcoming, and good buffet breakfasts.

Rosa et Al €€€ *Rua do Rosário 233; tel: 916 000 081;* www.rosaetal. pt. Close to the hip Bombarda quarter, this is an exclusive and much sought-after little boutique hotel in a converted townhouse. As well as comfortable, stylish rooms and a particularly good brunch there are cookery classes twice a week (very popular, book ahead), knitting and mindfulness retreats, a coffee shop, concept store and in-room spa service.

Torel Avantgarde €€€ *Rua da Restauração 336; tel: 220 110 082;* www. torelavantgarde.com. This new 5-star hotel is one of the hottest addresses in town. An art-lover's haven, it has 27 rooms and 20 suites named after famous avant-garde artists, writers, sculptors, architects and fashion designers, with decor reflecting the artist's personality and vision. Perched on the hillside, it has breathtaking views across the river to the wine lodges on the left bank. Confusingly, rooms come in 10 categories with wildly different prices, but all offering absolute comfort. The Digby restaurant, named after the English diplomat and philosopher who is known to have invented the modern wine bottle, offers contemporary Portuguese cuisine.

BOAVISTA

Hotel da Música €€ *Mercado do Bom Sucesso, Largo Ferreira Lapa; tel: 226 076 000;* www.hoteldamusica.com. Part of the revamped Mercado do Bom Sucesso, this 4-star designer hotel is an obvious choice for music lovers, close to the Casa da Música and with a musical theme throughout. It's also good for gourmets with all the culinary delights of the Mercado do Bom Sucesso on the doorstep. You can choose products from the market and have them cooked by the hotel's chef. It's a popular business hotel with reasonable prices but quite far from the centre.

VILA NOVA DE GAIA

Yeatman €€€€ *Rua do Choupelo, Vila Nova de Gaia; tel: 220 133 100;* www. the-yeatman-hotel.com. Strictly speaking the hotel is not in Porto, but across the river in Vila Nova de Gaia where there are very few hotels. However, once you are settled into this lap of luxury with its glorious river views, exceptional comfort, courteous service, Michelin-starred cuisine and fine port, you may not feel like moving very far. Named after Richard Yeatman, a member of the Taylor port family and author of the 1930 classic *1066 and All That*, the hotel sits above Taylor's port wine lodge, and port and wine are the name of the game: decanter-shaped swimming pool; spa therapies using extracts from the vine; Dick's Bar, with a wide choice of the finest wood-aged and Vintage Ports; a tour of the 25,000-bottle cellar; guest rooms individually designed by different wine producers; and one room where you can sleep inside an oak port vat!

FOZ DO DOURO

Hotel Boa-Vista €€ *Esplanada do Castelo 58, Foz do Douro; tel: 225 320 020;* www.hotelboavista.com. Combine seaside and city by staying at this traditional 3-star hotel in the suburb of Foz do Douro. Tram No. 1 and Bus No. 500 provide a good service along the waterfront into Porto. Built in 1900, the hotel lies across the road from the Fort of São João. Clean, comfortable rooms offer good value and there are fine views of the River Douro where it meets the sea from the front rooms, top-floor restaurant, pool and terrace.

INDEX

INSIGHT ⊙ GUIDES POCKET GUIDE

PORTO

First Edition 2019

Editor: Helen Fanthorpe
Author: Susie Boulton
Head of DTP and Pre-Press: Rebeka Davies
Picture Editor: Aude Vauconsant
Cartography: Carte
Photography Credits: Alamy 38, 55, 90; Arpad Radoczy/Picfair 26; Coelho/Epa/REX/Shutterstock 79; Daniel Rodrigues/Porto Convention & Visitors Bureau 100; Gary White/robertharding/REX/Shutterstock 92; Getty Images 1, 22, 56, 84, 94; iStock 4TC, 4MC, 4ML, 5M, 6L, 6R, 7, 17, 24, 29, 30, 33, 35, 37, 41, 45, 46, 49, 50, 52, 60, 72, 75, 77, 82, 83, 106; Luis Ferraz/Porto Convention & Visitors Bureau 65; Messias Delmar/Porto Convention & Visitors Bureau 63; Piano B 7R; Porto Convention & Visitors Bureau 5MC, 5M, 11, 13, 18, 21, 64; RUI PAULA - DOP RESTAURANTE - PORTO 14; Shutterstock 4TL, 5T, 5TC, 5MC, 43, 54, 58, 66, 68, 70, 76, 80, 87, 88, 99, 102, 104
Cover Picture: iStock

Distribution

UK, Ireland and Europe: Apa Publications (UK) Ltd; sales@insightguides.com
United States and Canada: Ingram Publisher Services; ips@ingramcontent.com
Australia and New Zealand: Woodslane; info@woodslane.com.au
Southeast Asia: Apa Publications (SN) Pte; singaporeoffice@insightguides.com
Worldwide: Apa Publications (UK) Ltd; sales@insightguides.com

Special Sales, Content Licensing and CoPublishing
Insight Guides can be purchased in bulk quantities at discounted prices. We can create special editions, personalised jackets and corporate imprints tailored to your needs. sales@insightguides.com; www.insightguides.biz

Contact us
Every effort has been made to provide accurate information in this publication, but changes are inevitable. The publisher cannot be responsible for any resulting loss, inconvenience or injury. We would appreciate it if readers would call our attention to any errors or outdated information. We also welcome your suggestions; please contact us at: hello@insightguides.com
www.insightguides.com

INSIGHT ⊙ GUIDES
OFF THE SHELF

Since 1970, INSIGHT GUIDES has provided a unique perspective on the world's best travel destinations by using specially commissioned photography and illuminating text written by local authors.

Whether you're planning a city break, a walking tour or the journey of a lifetime, our superb range of guidebooks and phrasebooks will inspire you to discover more about your chosen destination.

INSIGHT GUIDES
offer a unique combination of stunning photos, absorbing narrative and detailed maps, providing all the inspiration and information you need.

PHRASEBOOKS & DICTIONARIES
help users to feel at home, when away. Pocket-sized with a free app to download, they go where you do.

CITY GUIDES
pack hundreds of great photos into a smaller format with detailed practical information, so you can navigate the world's top cities with confidence.

EXPLORE GUIDES
feature easy-to-follow walks and itineraries in the world's most exciting destinations, with our choice of the best places to eat and drink along the way.

POCKET GUIDES
combine concise information on where to go and what to do in a handy compact format, ideal on the ground. Includes a full-colour, fold-out map.

EXPERIENCE GUIDES
feature offbeat perspectives and secret gems for experienced travellers, with a collection of over 100 ideas for a memorable stay in a city.

www.insightguides.com